LEADERSHIP ETHICS & SPIRITUALITY

A Christian Perspective

Revised Edition

J. Thomas Whetstone

Ordering Information:

For orders and inquiries, please contact:
1-888-375-9818
www.toplinkpublishing.com
bookorder@toplinkpublishing.com

Printed in the United States of America

Also by J. Thomas Whetstone:

The Manager as a Moral Person:
Exploring Paths to Excellence

A Southern Pioneer Woman

Light for the Dark Side:
Ethics Cases for University Administrators

CONTENTS

PART IV
GROWING AS A GOOD LEADER

APPENDIX
ESSAYS ON LEADERSHIP ISSUES

LIST OF EXHIBITS

DEDICATION

To the late Dr. John Reed Miller, my mentor and friend. A lifelong biblical scholar, a magnificent preacher, and a man of prayer, he always led effectively, ethically, and spiritually. He was a most gifted leader and teacher. After he had taught as a guest in one of my classes, a student rushed up to me to proclaim, "Thanks for inviting him to speak; this was the best class of the entire semester." I was duly humbled but had to agree.

PREFACE

The author proposes that leaders seriously apply biblical worldview concepts through a thoughtful Christian ethic. His intent is to offer leaders and future leaders practical guidance grounded in sound theory and biblical analysis.

Some might suggest that this optimistic purpose is too idealistic for the twenty-first century. Indeed, Paul Johnson (2003) observes that discontented intellectuals, the media, and those who seek a materialistic utopia on earth have cynically embraced an ideology of pessimism. Establishment spokespeople seem to say people can do nothing in the face of economic stagnation and decay, global warming, international terrorism, and political divisiveness.

Conservative theists correctly lament that American morals have been declining over recent decades. The Playboy philosophy of the 1950s seemed to give men permission to avoid the bonds of marriage in sexual practice. The birth control bill promoted sex without biological consequences. No-fault divorce nullified "until death us do part" from marriage commitments. Cohabitation, easily accessible pornography, and adoption of tolerance as the highest-priority value—except toward Christians and others holding to moral absolutes—have become ubiquitous. Cal Thomas (2010, 7) writes, "A nation that loses it moral sense is a nation without any sense at all." He further says that Muslim fanatics are right to condemn Western moral decay and materialism, although their solution—to impose Sharia law—is wrong.

However, the increasing moral darkness of our world should not diminish the hope of Christians; instead it challenges the faithful to gird their loins, for Christians called as leaders to demonstrate effective, ethical, and spiritual leadership. Such an optimistic response is fully justified. In God's perfect timing, Christ will return. Until then and always, God will reign supreme over His creation. Those who believe this tend to be optimists and often lead with assurance.

Humans are called as God's earthly stewards, and believers are created in Christ for good works, which God prepared beforehand, that we should walk in them (Ephesians 2:10). He wants His followers to be alert and ready and doing the duties for which they are called. Author Os Guinness tells of a 1780 session of the Connecticut House of Representatives that was interrupted when an unexpected eclipse of the sun occurred. Fear and clamor arose amidst the sudden darkness. Some members wanted to adjourn, some to pray, and some to prepare for the coming of the Lord. But the Speaker of the House rose to the occasion with sound logic and good faith, proclaiming, "The Day of the Lord is either approaching or it is not. If it is not, there is no cause for adjournment. And if the Lord *is* returning, I, for one, choose to be found doing my duty. I therefore ask that candles be brought" (Plantinga 2002, 144).

Christians always may trust their righteous, longsuffering, compassionate, and gracious God, regardless of differences in eschatological interpretations. Since all who are in Christ are to walk in the same manner as He walked (1 John 2:6), this clearly implies that those called as leaders should seek to lead as they understand Christ would if in their contextual roles. This book offers an outline for becoming a good leader who leads with technical competence and spiritual integrity. It is an imperfect attempt that admittedly is a work in progress. Questions are added to this revised edition to help guide individual self-examination and group discussion. The author's sincere hope is that this work will help each reader to lead wisely.

ACKNOWLEDGMENTS

This book would never have been written without the complete support of my wife and editor, Nancy Van Zant Whetstone. Her loving encouragement, insights, and repetitive—and demanding—editing corrections were magnificent. Dr. Byron Cherry graciously allowed me to include my articles in the appendix that I first published in his organization's online journal *Succeed to Lead*. Bonnie Schaefer provided invaluable assistance in the formulation of the study questions. I also commend the leaders I have served in my corporate management, ministerial, and academic workplaces. Although I have benefited from many exemplars, Dean Beth M. Doriani stands out as a truly ethical and spiritual leader of integrity, courage, and spirituality.

—J. Thomas Whetstone, DPhil

PART I

INTRODUCTION

Good leadership requires leaders who motivate others effectively to achieve good purposes. A good leader is one committed not only to grow in technical effectiveness but to apply a sound ethic with proper spiritual sensitivity. These high standards rest upon two basic tenets: (1) a good leader is both effective and ethical; and (2) the recognition of the importance of spirituality in business is increasing.

Chapter 1 offers a few general definitions and a rationale for why spirituality is important for a comprehensive leadership ethic and distinguishes biblical Christian spirituality from those of other worldview perspectives. The remainder of the book presents a reasoned Christian perspective of good leadership and practical suggestions as to how a person can become a better leader. It is not simply another how-to book, however, but posits leadership as a spiritual endeavor. This means a leader should seek to bridge the gap between her deeper, inner self and her ultimate source of calling, which for the Christian is the Triune God revealed in Scripture and Creation. Although the author addresses the subject from a particular spiritual worldview, that of orthodox Christianity, people of other faiths are encouraged to interact by contributing insights from their traditions.

CHAPTER 1

LEADERSHIP
AS A SPIRITUAL ENDEAVOR

*No society has ever flourished without a spiritual mission; the
quest for material progress alone is insufficient to spur men on
to the achievements which are required to create an enduring,
dynamic, progressive nation . . . . It is significant that the great
concern for more spirituality in business comes at a time when
our material progress has achieved extraordinary heights.—*
Arnold Toynbee, *A Study of History, 1934-1961*

The Need to Address Spiritual Values

Toynbee offered the above insight at Harvard Business School's
fiftieth anniversary conference, whose theme was "Management
Mission in a New Society" (quoted by Learned, Dooley, and Katz 1959,
113, as referenced in Flynn and Werhane 2008, 2). Every other speaker at
this conference likewise stressed the importance of giving more attention
to spiritual values.

Awareness of spirituality has increased, but after more than half
a century the worldwide financial crises of the twenty-first century
indicate a lack of progress integrating spirituality and leadership ethics.
Duska and Ragatz (2008) even argue that the contemporary malaise is
a corruption, the loss of soul—without a worthwhile defining purpose.
This may well account for much of the unethical behavior that so

scandalizes business and society today. Today's leaders thus need to think more deeply and seriously about applying spirituality and ethics within the global community.

This book seeks to present a reasoned Christian perspective of good leadership and practical suggestions as to how a person can lead well. Such leadership is a spiritual endeavor. A good leader seeks wholeheartedly to follow her ultimate source of calling, with expectation of success.

The Christian leader is called by God as a Christian and also as a leader, even if he does not fully understand or appreciate the role of God and the spiritual implications. To be a good leader, he must also learn to progress in effectiveness as a technically competent leader. A leader who is a Christian also needs to grow in his spiritual understanding according to a biblically based worldview and in his ability to apply a sound Christian ethic in the workplace.

Spirituality in Worldly Occupations

What is meant by "spirituality"? The *Concise Oxford Dictionary* (1990) defines "spiritual" as an adjective meaning (1) of or concerning the spirit as opposed to matter; (2) concerned with sacred or religious things; holy; divine; inspired. Spirituality can be conceived broadly as encompassing the aspects of the individual's search for inner peace and serenity; the significance of personal integrity and transparency; and mutual respect, trust, forgiveness, and love in our relationships. It also extends to concern for social justice and environmental stewardship and even to one's vision for the world and sense of personal calling in life (Dorr 2008).

Although the majority of people have some explicit or implicit vision of life that lies behind their more generous or less selfish actions and attitudes (Dorr 2008, 222), the Western mind tends to view *spiritual business* as an oxymoron. This reflects the dominant influence of the Enlightenment on modern and postmodern worldviews that restrict reality to the material. In contrast, an orthodox Christian's spiritual worldview requires an open-system perspective, one that recognizes meaning in other levels of reality beyond naturalism, materialism, determinism, and secular humanism.

Scientists such as Michael Polanyi realize humans cannot be fully explained materialistically in terms of their physical bodies and brain cells. Life operates by principles *made possible* and *limited* by physical and chemical laws but not *determined by them* (Scott 1995). Polanyi sees natural science as pointing beyond intelligible nature to a higher realm of communion with the divine personhood (Kelly 2008; Torrance 1984). Openness to spirituality is thus a rational means for seeking meaning to human rationality and consciousness.

Humanist Understandings

However, Enlightenment thinking has objected to such interpretations, and logical positivists (e.g., Bertrand Russell and Willard Quine) insist that various levels of reality are closed off within themselves without being open to higher levels. Such denial of any meaningful influence from beyond humanity ultimately leads to the existentialist conclusion that life is absurd.

More optimistic are those distinguished leaders whom Lawrence Carter Sr. designates as "spiritually aware visionary activists." Carter includes in this group John Shelby Spong, Joseph Campbell, Daisaku Ikeda, Deepak Chopra, Martin Luther King Jr., Mahatma Gandhi, the Dalai Lama, Andrew Cohen, Betty L. Siegel, and Derek Bok. Their vision is "to awaken humanity to its spiritual magnificence" (Carter 2007, 142) "to allow more people to take a quantum jump to a place to build a world of peace, reconciliation, and connectedness" (Carter 2007, 143). For such universalist humanists, the "soulful excellence of leadership" transcends religious law sanctioned by the church or God, civil law sanctioned by the state, and natural law sanctioned by intelligence, instead resting squarely on ethical laws or principles sanctioned by rational will (Carter 2007, 138).

Carter seeks to explain that spiritually aware, ethically based leadership raises people (at least partly through education) to live as global citizens, universal humans, and planetary incarnations (Carter 2007, 141). It is Ikeda's "interdependent co-arising of all things" (Carter 2007, 142). "When you cooperate with ultimate good, you become one with Infinite Spirit. We are one with nature, people, plants, and animals in their hunger, pain, and pleasure" (Carter 2007, 143). This is a pantheistic understanding, one that stems more from David Thoreau's transcendentalism than from orthodox Christianity.

5

Notably, such modernist, universalist humanism tends to elevate human collective will over what Christians believe is divine revelation. Lawrence Carter even claims that spiritual growth is often held back because of literal translations of sacred texts. "To grow spiritually, I believe we have to stop quoting scripture, any sacred scripture, as evidence of our beliefs, and start looking for the deeper meaning that these sacred stories hold, what James W. Fowler (1981) calls 'Universalizing Faith'" (Carter 2007, 138-39).

Christian Spirituality

Rather than presuming to create a spiritual perspective, Christian humanists instead recognize spiritual values as a gift of God. As T. S. Eliot said, "Man is man because he can recognize spiritual realities, not because he can invent them" (quoted by Birzer 2012, 40). "In our hour of crisis the key to real power, to the command of reality which the higher imagination gives, remains the fear of God" (Russell Kirk 1963, as quoted by Birzer 2012, 40).

Moreover, Christians can recognize that human hubris is extremely dangerous. This is a deeper meaning of the story in Genesis 11. When all the earth's people worked collectively to build the Tower of Babel to "reach into heaven," God was not pleased. Ignoring or subordinating God's revealed will, even for goals seeming admirable to visionary leaders, is ill advised. A Christian humanist instead views God-given spirituality as beneficial if accepted as governing. A Christian worldview holds that Scripture is believers' perfect rule of faith and practice. "Man shall not live on bread alone, but on every word that proceeds out of the mouth of God" (Deuteronomy 8:3; Matthew 4:4). Christians, whether leaders or followers, expect to benefit from holding to Paul's teaching as recorded in 2 Timothy 3:16-17: "All Scripture is inspired by God and profitable for teaching, for reproof, for correction, for training in righteousness; that the man of God may be adequate, equipped for every good work."

However, is scriptural adherence realistic, even practical, for today's worldly and pluralistic workplace? Yes, if the reader realizes that the Bible cannot be used as one's textbook for leadership any more than as an engineering manual. A Christian leader also needs to study and apply the findings of research and learn from his or her experience and that of others. Indeed, Christian spirituality must involve recognition and response to God's general revelation through study of nature as well as to special revelation as reported throughout Scripture (especially note Psalms 19, 29, and 135). This book thus draws extensively from leadership research and theories that can help the reader consider how to develop as an effective and ethical leader in his or her chosen occupation.

Indeed, while a biblical Christian worldview provides the control beliefs (see Wolterstorff 1984, 70) for testing ethical leadership theories and practices, Scripture is not the believer's sole or even primary literary source. As Cappadocian Father Basil the Great wrote in the fourth century AD, Christians can make use of pagan classics (which may be based on heathen mythology and pagan ethics) in the education of their youth if Christian writings and practice provide the standard of selectivity (Basil 1965). A spiritual orientation should not narrow the leader's view but instead broaden it to include scientific and mathematical truths about the natural functioning of the universe and social relationships. How then should we understand *leadership*?

Leadership

Most simply, a leader is one who has followers (Smith 1986); he moves others to do something. Nevertheless, amidst the complexities of human interrelationships, "leadership remains an intriguing but elusive phenomenon" (Leavy 2008, 103). Leaders are very diverse; this is why Leavy objects that attributes such as emotional intelligence (Goleman 2004) or tough-minded humility (Collins 2001) fall short of providing full insight into the essence of outstanding leadership, especially at the organizational level (Leavy 2008, 103-4). Context gives vision real meaning for people; without context, a vision is a fantasy (Leavy 2008). A compelling vision tends to be rooted in values, convictions, and principles of a more transcendent nature, directed toward some good telos, an impersonal final purpose in the Aristotelian sense or according to the Trinitarian God of Christianity.

Ethics and Leadership

Ethics is an integral aspect of the above understanding of leadership. John Knapp states that *"good* leadership requires more than just effectiveness in getting things done. It is as much about who leaders are as what they do. And it is about the ends they value and the means they choose to pursue them" (Knapp 2007, xii). At the personal level, business ethics (indeed, any occupational ethic) considers standards for good versus bad, right versus wrong, and the virtuous versus vicious behavior of individuals working in industry, finance, and other activities. At the institutional level, it is concerned with the institutional responsibilities and behaviors of organizations. More widely conceived, business ethics addresses the role and responsibilities of business in global society, public policy relating to business, and society's long-term attitudes to and shifting expectations of business and the corporate world.

From an open-system perspective, behavior at all these levels can be influenced by spiritual forces within individuals and society. People act subject to both the immanent influences and transcendant standards of something supernatural. Without a rich understanding of the moral and spiritual implications of what people do in their businesses, they misunderstand their contribution to the wider society and ultimately lose perspective of their very selves and their companies (Naughton and Cornwall 2009, 3).

Modern culture hinders or even blocks the development of full-orbed leadership qualities because of the artificial separation between ethics and spirituality (Verstraeten 2008, 132). The cave of Plato can serve as a metaphor for the limited hermeneutical horizon in which today's managers and business ethicists operate: they refuse to be interrupted or disturbed by a perspective different from their own, sticking to their narrow interpretation of reality. According to Verstraeten, leadership has become problematic because of (1) the impossibility of interpreting the sphere of work as meaningful; (2) the fragmentation of conscience; (3) the lack of interior life; and (4) the manipulation of the soul. The solution to these obstacles is more than a matter of ethics; as a precondition for leadership, one must mobilize one's imagination and spirituality as preconditions for innovative thinking and autonomous innovative action (Verstraeten 2008).

Spirituality and Ethical Leadership

At its deepest, spirituality as a prerequisite to leadership is an act of faith, a response subsequent to external spiritual intervention—although it is not to be confused with fideism (Kelly 2008, 117). For the Christian believer, acting in faith requires one to repent and entrust oneself to ultimate acceptance by God. Even for the atheist, spiritual leadership is an act of faith: the refusal of ultimate meaninglessness and an apparent leap of faith in the rejection of nihilism. In spite of his initial experience of absurdity, the nonbeliever's protest against the latter serves to open him to a horizon of new possibilities (Verstraeten 2008).

Nevertheless, leaders of all persuasions often overlook the spiritual dimension in their pressured rush toward pragmatism. Business people, for example, can seek profitability as the ultimate "bottom line," as opposed to viewing it as an important (even commendable) means to more meaningful ends. In the United States, even openly confessing Christians can often be described as dualists (Nash and McLennan 1991), projecting one lifestyle in church and home but at work conforming to the rough and tumble pragmatism they associate with competitive business (Carr 1968).

But an ethical and spiritual leader should not be controlled and determined by compulsions for workaholism or pleasing other humans, whether organizational superiors, peers, subordinates, or other stakeholders. She is to remain genuinely free to trust and follow that to which she is called most profoundly.

A Christian Perspective for Leadership Ethics

The working definition developed in this book is that *an ethical and spiritually minded leader is a person of strong character virtues who seeks to influence followers and the organization toward a good purpose in a principled manner.* For a Christian to practice leadership as a spiritual endeavor, he or she must possess genuine Christian faith, as well as a sense of calling to leadership. He also needs a capacity for ethical reflection and technical competency in leadership knowledge and skills that he can apply according to a biblical worldview. Although good leaders can adhere to different faiths, this book relies on the author's understanding of an explicitly Christian open-system approach to exemplify how spirituality can be practiced by leaders in the workplace. The perspective of this book is thus Christian.

Admittedly, using a particular religious focus, such as biblical Christianity, can disturb people who are more comfortable speaking of moral and spiritual values that have no particular religious or denominational character. But what should disturb spiritually aware people even more is the risk of a naturalistic, closed system practice of handling the challenges of the new entrepreneurial economy with only economic and political resources or generic calls for values that are ultimately unhinged from anything that is concrete (Naughton and Cornwall 2009). Leaders must be ever mindful of the worst abuses of religion but also must be mindful of a very important truth about life: humans are at their best when they speak from their center, not from their boundaries —and they tend to compromise their lives when they lose sight of this center (Fortin 2006). In this book, the spiritual center chosen is Jesus Christ. Without drifting from their center, Christians should develop as ethical leaders not only by applying insights from research and experience but also as they are guided spiritually by God's revelation in Scripture.

Questions for Discussion:

1. Is is really necessary that a leader be ethical in order to be a good leader? Explain why or why not.
2. Is a spiritually-minded person more likely to lead ethically on a consistent basis than one unfocused on spiritual concerns? Why or why not? Can you support your answer from personal observation and experience?
3. In what ways can a person be influenced by and apply his spiritually in his business or profession? Offer examples.
4. Is it fair to criticize a person for leading according to a different ethic at work than the one he or she portrays in church on Sunday?
5. Should a Christian use leadership models and approaches (such as systems thinking or positive psychology) that have been developed by non-Christians or atheists? Explain your answer.

6. In this book, holding an open systems view requires a person to acknowledge the possibility of meaningful influences of something beyond natural and material forces of nature. In other words, the person believes in supernatural power over events and circumstances. Identify examples, if any, of supernatural influence that you have witnessed.

PART II

THE GOOD LEADER—
EFFECTIVE, ETHICAL, AND
SPIRITUALLY MINDED

*H*ow does one become a spiritually engaged ethical leader? This book seeks answers from an orthodox Christian perspective. Adapting Joanne Ciulla's (2004) description of a good leader as being both ethical and effective, it proposes that a Christian, if called to a leadership role, should apply a biblical worldview to becoming a good leader—one who is effective, ethical, *and* spiritually minded. Part II discusses effective, ethical leadership (chapter 2) and adds to it the open-system perspective of spiritual leadership (chapter 3).

CHAPTER 2

EFFECTIVE, ETHICAL LEADERSHIP

*So he shepherded them according to the integrity of his heart,
and guided them with his skillful hands.* —Psalm 78:72

To be effective, a leader needs to practice the skills and employ styles and models confirmed by research and his personal experience and context as he leads others. Moreover, an effective Christian leader behaves according to a sound biblical ethic. This chapter develops this understanding of leadership effectiveness. But first, it considers how *leadership* should be defined.

What Is Leadership?

"Defining leadership is simple: a leader is one who has followers," according to businessman and consultant Fred Smith (1986). Nevertheless, he acknowledges that performing as a leader is anything but easy. "Leader" is not a title but a function, a skill to perform, and a service to render for the whole group (Smith 1986). The very way one defines leadership further contains within it normative assumptions as to leader-follower relationships (Ciulla 2004). Leadership concerns how persons move others to do something. The GLOBE researchers, in their worldwide leadership study, support this basic understanding, defining leadership as "the ability of an individual to influence, motivate, and enable others to contribute toward the effectiveness and success of the organization of which they are members" (House et al. 2004, 15). The character of the leader is critically important; as Frances Hesselbein observes, "leadership is about how to be, not how to do" (Knapp 2007, xv).

Leadership can be studied as a science but must also be recognized as an art (Banks and Ledbetter 2004), or an ensemble of arts (Grint 2000). It is a subject imbued with intangibles. To ensure followers actually follow, leaders need to combine the creative with the professional, the visionary with the logistical, the entrepreneurial with the managerial—to establish identity, formulate strategic vision, construct organizational tactics, and deploy persuasive mechanisms. Genuine leaders expect and are at home with ambiguity, paradox, and even contradiction (Banks and Ledbetter 2004, 26). March and Weil (2005) see leadership as both plumbing and poetry. Leadership proficiency requires use of known techniques, competence in everyday tasks, careful delegation and follow-up, and a shared sense of community—all based on and nurturing security and trust. As poetry, leadership explores unexpected avenues, seeking meaning and how to communicate it, thus adding adventure and rendering life interesting and attractive. The act of leading can be seen as a process that evolves and develops over time.

The traditional view of leaders in social and business organizations is that they set direction, make the important decisions, and rally the followers (usually fellow employees) (Senge 1990). Top leaders are visionary decision makers (e.g., Steven Jobs of Apple Computer, Bill Gates of Microsoft, and Jeff Bezos of Amazon.com). The CEO decides where to go, and then, through a combination of persuasion and edict, directs others in the process of implementation (Nutt 1989). But the increasingly global business environment of multi-business organizations has made the top management task more complex. Varied situations may require different leadership approaches—pointing to flexibility and contingency leadership (Harrison et al. 2010, 66). The CEO's most important role is to harness the energy, talents, and creativity of the individuals who make up the organization (Harrison et al. 2010, 66).

The literature on leadership is overwhelming and seems to expand exponentially, as a quick survey of libraries, bookstores, and the Internet can quickly reveal. Although James MacGregor Burns (1978) observes that leadership is "one of the most observed and least understood phenomena on earth," this cannot be blamed on a lack of academic attention. Leadership books and theories abound and are continually published. A 2009 search of the Business Source Complete database of academic journals found more than twenty-seven thousand articles using the term *leadership*.

This chapter includes a relatively brief overview of the academic research on leadership. This summary, which may seem rather dry reading to some, provides a background that can not only provide information but shows that leadership, even as an academic subject, is too dynamic, complex, and challenging to be fully grasped by rigorous scientific study. Even mastering the research cannot teach a person how to be a good leader. Perhaps more is learned by observing and meeting effective leaders; reading their biographies, autobiographies, and interviews for clues; and deciding existentially which insights a person can emulate or adapt for his own leadership approach, followers, and situation. For example, Dr. James Watson, discoverer of the double helix and warrior against cancer, says, "To be a good leader you generally have to ruffle feathers," which he believes most people are unwilling to do (Finley 2010, A15). Though not a comprehensive or universal definition in the academic sense, this brings out an aspect absent from the research literature. A sample of other definitions of leadership is offered in exhibit 1. An aspiring leader would be wise to watch and listen for such opinions as he forms and lives according to his own understanding.

There is no universal definition of leadership because it is viewed and studied in different ways that require different definitions (Lussier and Achua 2010). Most academics and successful leaders seem to agree, however, that leadership is the influencing process of leaders and followers to achieve organizational objectives through change (Lussier and Achua 2010, 6). Influence is the essence of leadership (Clark 2007, 48). The working definition developed in this book is that *an ethical and spiritually minded leader is a person of strong character virtues who seeks to influence followers and the organization toward a good purpose in a principled manner.* This is symbolized on the book cover by the torch, scales, and heart; an effective, ethical, and spiritually-minded leader competently carries the torch of leadership using ethically balanced means, because his character (sanctified heart) disposes him to do so.

EXHIBIT 1
WHAT DO LEADERS SAY?

Leadership is influence, the ability of one person to influence others. One man can lead others only to the extent that he can influence them to follow his lead.—J. Oswald Sanders (1994)

Leadership is the capacity and will to rally men and women to a common purpose, and the character which inspires confidence.—Lord Bernard Montgomery

A leader is a person who has the ability to get others to do what they don't want to do, and like it.—President Harry S. Truman

Follow me!—Motto of the US Army Infantry School, Ft. Benning, GA

Leadership is work—not traits or qualities and not charisma. It is a responsibility, not a privilege. Trust is essential. It is being a trumpet with a clear sound.—Peter Drucker

The leader leads by a superior knowledge, a dominating personality, knowledge of the job, grasp of the total situation.—Mary Parker Follett

[A person can lead] if you can find that peace within yourself, that peace and quiet and confidence that you can pass on to others, so that they know that you are honest and you are fair and will help them, no matter what, when the chips are down.—Major Dick Winters, commander of Easy Company, 101st Airborne Division, "The Band of Brothers"

Leading Well Is Not Easy

People in leadership roles naturally desire that their followers and others value them as good leaders, or at least as effective ones. But their followers might not always do so. Satirist Scott Adams says that organizations where he worked were riddled with "hamster-brained sociopaths in leadership roles" and "Our system requires a continuous supply of highly capable people who are so disgruntled with their jobs that they are willing to chew off their own arms to escape their bosses. The economy needs hamster-brained sociopaths in management to drive down the opportunity cost of entrepreneurship. Luckily, we're blessed with an ample supply..." (Adams 2010, C3).

Developing a practical understanding of the *how* of leading well is a more difficult and more interesting challenge than merely defining leadership. Indeed, a problem with the literature is the dearth of study addressing *ethical leadership* (Ciulla 2006). For example, Bass and Stodhill's Handbook (1990), the standard reference on leadership, has thirty-seven chapters on leadership but none on ethics, though ethics is the heart of leadership (Ciulla 2005, 19). Effective leadership calls for ethical leadership and is also a spiritual endeavor.

Christian managers and leaders are not exempt from Adams's satirical critique and would be wise to consider it. Genuine spirituality is necessary for the person with an open-system worldview, but it is not enough for the leader. Moreover, a Christian may even seek to apply a reasoned, biblically grounded ethic and still fail as a leader if he lacks the skills and characteristics of an effective leader that apply to his particular role, followers, and situation. Leadership is not only a spiritual endeavor but a process in the natural sphere of social organizations. Spiritually minded and ethically oriented leaders should also grow in practical leadership effectiveness. This requires that they apply appropriate leadership skills learned through cognitive study and hands-on experience.

The Effective Leader

Stakeholders have very high expectations for organizational leaders. The specific challenges a leader faces can vary in nature and difficulty, but can be grouped into four core responsibilities: fulfilling the mission, obeying the law, being ethical, and exhibiting good citizenship (Carroll 2009). An effective leader should seek to perform with excellence in each of these core areas.

Leaders must assure that the organization has a clear understanding and commitment to a mission. Stakeholders should be able to agree that "this is the business we are in and it is an appropriate one." A leader must have and diligently exercise the set of skills and qualities that effectuate the mission— that move the organization successfully toward it. He is responsible for shepherding the mission and preventing activities contrary to the mission. At the same time, he is the primary agent for initiating and gaining acceptance to modifications or major directional changes to the mission, plans, and implementation strategies due to new opportunities and threats that he continually and actively seeks to see or foresee.

Promotion of an Ethical Culture

The effective leader promotes an organizational culture that values obedience to all laws that govern the people and activities of the organization. Cultural integrity (Paine 1994) depends on compliance with God's law and society's law and government regulations. The leader potentially controls the most powerful means for embedding and reinforcing legal and other cultural values. He influences legal obedience by his personal example and properly humble exercise of his authority for the common good. The primary culture-forming mechanisms available to the leader are (1) what he pays attention to, measures, and controls; (2) his reactions to critical incidents and organizational crises; (3) deliberate role modeling; (4) criteria for allocation of rewards and status; and (5) criteria for recruitment, selection, promotion, retirement, and excommunication (Edgar Schein 1985).

Leadership excellence sets the bar higher than legal compliance, effectiveness, and efficiency in achieving organizational objectives. Today, leaders are expected to lead by excellence and ethics (Carroll 2009, 101). Leaders who display extraordinary ethics are honest, trustworthy, dedicated, wise, and accountable, and keep their promises (ibid.). Empirical research (Whetstone 2003) ranks honesty as the highest of the required manager virtues in a grocery chain, whereas the dishonest manager is considered the worst, most vicious, of all. Dishonesty and lack of trust are dysfunctional for the team, the firm, and society. Establishing and maintaining trust is essential for the ethical organization, and as Max De Pree states, "Leadership is barren and hollow when it does not have integrity at its core" (Banks and Ledbetter 2004, 9).

Leaders are also expected to serve as role models of enthusiastic community service. Archie Carroll (2009, 101) says good citizenship "is the icing on the cake for effective leaders." Through his volunteerism and sacrifice, the leader should promote an ethos of putting others before self. This of course is essential for having and encouraging others to live and work according to a moral sense, as opposed to a natural self-centeredness. William May even calls on business leaders to possess not only the traditional virtues of industry, honesty, and integrity, and the cooperative virtues that render one artful in acting in relationship with others, but also substantially and preeminently public spiritedness (May 1987, 694).

The leader needs to know where he or she is and be confident that he or she is seeking a good purpose (or *telos*). But this is not enough. He or she must take responsibility to work within the organization, influencing others in the right way, with moral integrity according to principled obligations. He must believe the mission is achievable and uphold its viability. If the mission puts customers first, the leader must assure that members throughout the organization do as well. If the mission commits to producing quality products and providing exemplary service, he is responsible for setting cultural values that employ the right methods and for seeing that the organization provides the necessary structural and resource support for followers.

Especially in larger organizations, cultural formation only starts with the leader. It can be established and fully embedded by the joint efforts of often widely dispersed subordinates and local leaders. The top leaders should commit to what Joanne Ciulla (2004) calls genuine empowerment, requiring proper delegation of decision-making authority and responsibility; realization of a mutual understanding and identification with the mission with followers and other stakeholders; the obligation to obey the law; the essential importance of ethical conduct; and the practice of good citizenship. This suggests the need for a normative view of leadership that emphasizes the relational, that the leader is a person of influence in relationship with his followers. These responsibilities are closely identified with normative theories such as transformational and servant leadership (which will be discussed later).

But ethical behavior relies more on the character of the leader and the example he sets than on the leadership style he adopts.

Each leader is a uniquely different individual. Everyone is blessed with relative strengths and relative weaknesses and faces opportunities and situations that differ and change, often dramatically, over a lifetime. A leader needs to grow and adapt his or her individual style and develop the needed technical skills and practices as he seeks to meet his responsibilities with effectiveness in his organizational or social context. For this, an effective leader must be a student of others, his occupation, the internal environment of his organization, the external environment of his industry, and the global political economy. This is no one-off task; throughout his career he should continue to examine himself and adapt to approaches that best suit his various strengths and minimize the detrimental effects of his weaknesses as he matures as a leader.

The following section reviews some major findings of leadership research. Understanding the progress made by social scientists over the past century provides a cognitive, though partial, foundation for the person to formulate his own approach to leadership. The interested reader might also further investigate the academic subject of leadership, perhaps starting with the referenced sources. The chapter concludes with a brief description of a good leader—one who is both effective and ethical. The next chapter more directly addresses the spiritual dimension of leadership. Later chapters build on the concepts presented in parts I and II to develop an integrated description of an effective, ethical, and spiritually minded leader based on a biblical Christian worldview perspective.

Conceptual Developments from Management and Leadership Research

Over the past century, academics have sought to understand more about how leaders actually behave and how they should best behave (see Lussier and Achua 2010). Modern research on management and leadership initially was primarily scientific and descriptive. In recent years, it has increasingly made room for paradigms such as transformational and servant leadership that deliberately address the moral character and purpose of leaders and followers. Researchers' descriptions and analyses can appear misdirected and too limited when viewed in retrospect, but they more importantly highlight the complexity of this multidimensional subject—which in practical application is both an art and a science.

Early twentieth-century research concentrated on the manager or leader himself, seeking to find universal behavioral responsibilities and traits for maximizing work efficiency. Based on its anthropological presuppositions, scientific management sought to determine the most efficient work processes, which the manager or leader could prescribe for workers to follow. Frederick Taylor (1916) and others of the scientific management school believed the manager was responsible for engineering work processes and then directing his followers how to work in the most productive manner. Henri Fayol (1916) identified universal principles, such as unity of command and delegation of authority equal to responsibility, none of which any manager or leader could ignore without substantial cost. Max Weber (1947) promoted bureaucracy as an organizational design based on merit and competency, one he thought best overcame the inefficiencies of placing managers in offices based on social position or other forms of favoritism.

Scientific management thinkers contributed significantly to workplace productivity but tended to depersonalize followers and discount the importance of social relationships of people working together. Mary Parker Follett (1924) was an exception, emphasizing the practical contributions of followers who could guide and correct leaders who listened. Early leadership research sought to identify the traits characteristic of successful leaders. However, Great Man or Trait theories were largely abandoned by the late 1940s because different leaders, including those with recognized success, tend to have different distinctive traits. Leadership scholars began to believe that the best approach of leadership depends on the contextual situation and the followers as well as on any set of qualities of the leader (Bass 1990). For example, behavioral theory can focus empirically on what the leader does and says rather than on personality traits—which are more difficult to quantify.

Behavioral researchers identified two basic leader styles: (1) job-centered (high concern for production); or (2) employee-centered (high concern for people). Behavioral research also has provided the basis for a number of motivation theories. Blake and Mouton (1984) used these style dimensions to develop the Managerial Grid and Questionnaire that evolved into the Leadership Grid (Blake and McCanse 1991) to allow people to locate themselves in one of five leadership styles:

- Impoverished (low concern for production and people)
- Authority Compliance (high concern for production and low for people)
- Country Club (low concern for production and high concern for people)
- Middle of the Road
- Team Leader (high concern for production and people)

Extensive empirical testing indicates that the combination style of high concern for production and high concern for people, which Blake and McCanse recommend, is not only difficult to achieve but is not always the most effective in different situations. In fact, no behavioral theory has yet achieved the goal of finding the one best leadership style for all situations— the optimal combination of traits, skills, and behaviors. No leadership behaviors can consistently be associated with leader effectiveness with followers (Miner 2003).

Although most scholars no longer seek to identify universal characteristics that every leader must possess, some recent research on leader traits does contribute to leadership understanding. The widely accepted Big Five Model of Personality Traits (Judge, Heller, and Mount 2002) classifies personal qualities into the dimensions of

- surgency (dominant; competitive; influencing);
- agreeableness (warm; sociable);
- adjustment (emotional stability);
- conscientiousness (achievement focused; dependable); and
- openness to experience (nonconforming; willing to change).

People high in surgency generally are perceived as leader-like. They work hard and seek change more than they like to please everyone. They generally are stable emotionally, being good under pressure, relaxed, secure, and positive (Lussier and Achua 2010, 35). Researchers also identify nine traits that consistently differentiate leaders from others (Lussier and Achua 2010):

- dominance
- high energy
- self-confidence
- internal locus of control
- emotional stability
- integrity (honesty and trustworthiness)
- cognitive intelligence
- emotional intelligence
- flexibility
- sensitivity to others

Whereas these traits may represent general tendencies, it is important to recognize that every person is a unique creation; proven leaders can vary in the particular traits they manifest. For example, George Washington, acclaimed by his contemporaries as "first in war, first in peace, and first in the hearts of his countrymen," was prone to lose his temper.

Fiedler developed the first contingency leadership theory to investigate how situational variables interact with leader personality and behavior. Believing each person has a dominant leadership style, either high task or high relationship, he said the leader should seek a situation that best suits his dominant style. For this, the leader should consider the situational variables of relationship with his followers, the nature of the task, and his relative position power (Fiedler 1967). If the situation does not match the leader's style, the leader seeks to change the situation or find a new situation that better fits. Later situational/contingency theories instead assume that leaders can change their style to meet the situation. The Path-Goal Leadership Theory and Model (House and Mitchell 1974) can be used by a leader to select his most appropriate style based on the employees' perceptions of their goals and the paths they follow to achieve them.

The Normative Leadership Theory and Model (Vroom and Jago 1988) is an even more complex model a person can use to select his followers' level of participation in a decision—the leader decides, consults individually, consults group, facilitates, or delegates to followers. Many academics approve the normative model because it is well-researched; managers using the model-recommended style have a 62 percent probability of making a successful decision (Lussier and Achua 2010, 170). However, managers tend to find it too cumbersome to be very practical.

Overall, the descriptive academic research seems to reach a consensus that considerate leaders usually have more satisfied subordinates (Yukl 1989). But this is not a very satisfying result to come from such extensive academic investigation. How does this really help those who sincerely seek to learn how to develop into good leaders? According to Joanne Ciulla (2006), the problem is that the scientific research neglects or ignores moral implications. If ethics is the heart of leadership, as she contends, normative assumptions concerning the leader-follower relationships are needed. This means that management and leadership research has been too narrow in scope. Whereas scientific leadership research is positivist, focused on traits, behaviors, skills, and group facilitation, and seeks to break leadership into components that can be analyzed, ethical analysis is necessarily more broad and contextual as it attempts to meet its challenges regarding trust, stakeholders, and values in a society of diverse human beings.

In recent years researchers have increased their focus on the relationships between leaders and followers. Dyadic theory attempts to explain why leaders vary their behavior with different followers. Transactional leadership involves an exchange of valued benefits, based on values and motivations of both leaders and followers. The leader rewards specific behaviors and performance and somehow punishes those who fail to meet his expectations. Leader-member exchange theory (LMX) finds that employees who perceive themselves to be in supportive relationships with their supervisors tend to have higher performance, job satisfaction, and organizational commitment (Liden et al. 2006). A growing acknowledgment of the crucial importance of trust for successful leader-follower relationships, as well as for good team dynamics, has set the stage for normative approaches that consider moral character concerns.

Leadership Theories That Focus on Purpose and Moral Character

Charismatic and transformational leadership theories return the focus to the leader, viewing the leader and his followers as moral persons seeking meaning. They transform the needs, aspirations, and values of followers from self-interest to collective interest, they practice trust building to create a strong mission commitment, and they generate excitement, emotion, and energy that cause followers to be willing to sacrifice beyond merely a sense of duty. But charismatic leaders are not necessarily morally good leaders, and it can be unwise to follow and emulate them simply because they are charismatic (Lussier and Achua 2010, 345). Adolf Hitler was certainly charismatic. The values and personality of the leader and his real purpose, his own needs, or the needs of the followers and the organization must be considered (Jung and Sosik 2006).

Transformational Leadership

Transformational leadership (Burns 1978; Bass and Steidlmeier 2004) is a widely touted normative theory that emphasizes the ethical influence of leaders, who are often—but not always—charismatic. Transformational leaders such as Winston Churchill, Mahatma Gandhi, and Aung San Suu Kyi transform the lives and characters of their followers and societies. They use their charisma and inspirational motivation to challenge followers to be creative in problem solving, focusing on communicating a vision of the future that followers come to share and seek. Transformational leaders may employ transactional techniques such as substantive rewards but primarily seek to motivate by appealing to their followers' higher ideals and moral values. In theory, a transformational leader aspires to raise the level of morality of her followers and of the organization, creating a more moral climate, fostering independent action, and serving the greater good. Moreover, transformational leadership can effectively succeed in increasing the economic performance of subordinates, which is a major reason for its popularity (Johnson 2001). Many recent books written by successful organizational leaders elaborate a form of transformational leadership based on their particular experience. The approach of Kouzes and Posner (2004) recommending that the leader model the way, inspire a shared vision, challenge the process, enable others to act, and encourage the heart is a prime example.

Like any leadership approach, transformational leadership involves risks, given the reality of mankind's fall into sinfulness. Followers can grow dependent on the leader as their charismatic hero (Johnson 2001). The pragmatic effectiveness of this approach can encourage the leader to downplay the contributions of his followers in order to promote his own interests (Kelley 1992). Rightly or not, over time followers can come to suspect the leader of manipulation, using them for his own purposes rather than respecting them as worthy ends in themselves. The greatest risk is that the leader might use transformational techniques for immoral ends. Attila the Hun, Napoleon Bonaparte, and Adolf Hitler can be understood as being effective transformational leaders. Whereas transformational leadership emphasizes the development of character within followers toward a purposeful vision, that end may be good or bad, and the followers may lack the principled constraints as to how that vision is pursued (Whetstone 2002). Keeley (1995) explains that by combining pragmatism with enculturation of moral (or immoral) vision, this paradigm places inadequate stress on individual rights and moral duties required to guide behaviors toward genuine communal good.

Admittedly, Bass and Steidlmeier (2004) disagree with this assessment. While acknowledging the "Hitler problem" and other criticisms, these proponents of transformational leadership distinguish between *transformational* and *pseudo-transformational* leaders: whereas the latter are self-centered, genuine transformational leaders are motivated by altruism. In leadership, character matters (Bass and Steidlmeier 2004, 185). Hitler may have excelled in applying transformational practices, but according to Bass, he was not a genuine transformational leader.

But transformational leadership does incorporate spiritual concerns (which can be good or evil) such as relational dynamics, vision, and values into leadership thinking and practice. A transformational leader can be effective in instilling a vision, molding the character and vision of followers, and motivating them toward its achievement. This involves moral risks, which increase with the leader's effectiveness. If the vision is flawed or if the leader or followers neglect to ensure that behaviors toward that vision are morally principled, the results can be tragic (Rasmussen 1995, 297).

Servant Leadership

Servant leadership seeks to develop moral character and meaning by focusing on the leader and his personal nature as he carries out the role of steward and servant of the people and the organization. This normative theory aims for a culture of spiritual growth whereas transformational leadership leads to an empowered dynamic culture (Smith, Montagno and Kuzmenko 2004). The leader as servant puts his primary emphasis on the needs and desires of the followers before his own needs and desires (Greenleaf 1977). There is no unique formula for the servant leader's behaviors; he waits and listens to his followers to define them. His preferred methods are persuasion and example and he measures success by the growth in the people he serves and by benefits to the common good.

Scripture depicts Jesus Christ as a sacrificial, loving servant leader (e.g., Matthew 20:28), and many Christians look to servant leadership as the optimal paradigm for ethical leadership and spirituality. Nevertheless, as a theory and as practiced by imperfect humans, servant leadership has also received criticism. A later chapter further assesses servant leadership.

The Good Leader

An effective and ethical leader not only must communicate a clear vision and purpose for followers, she also must exhibit the moral character to honor the rights of others while fulfilling her own obligations in a principled, knowledgeable, and skillful manner. Leadership is developed as people are challenged, even thrust into new and difficult situations. As Aristotle taught, habits can develop and virtue can be honed by acting virtuously. After the learner makes mistakes, a mentor often provides support, encouraging persistence toward improvement. Furthermore, as in moral character development, ethical leaders develop as they seek to emulate behaviors that role models set for them. A good leader may also be an effective mentor, someone who develops others into good leaders, preserving the line of those who fit well.

The person who has invested the time and the serious thoughtful effort to understand his worldview will be more likely to apply it consistently when decisions must be made. Because pressures and temptations are ever present in the world, where complex interactions of often competing responsibilities can make consistent worldview practice very challenging, the leader needs to build upon basic worldview thinking by applying thoughtful biblically based ethical analysis. From an open system worldview perspective, a good leader thus needs to be spiritually minded as well as effective and ethical. The spiritually oriented leader not only seeks to serve effectively according to sound ethics, but also seriously undertakes a responsibility to offer his followers and others support in finding meaning and purpose.

The next chapter focuses on the leader's spiritual role in the workplace and some practical ways for addressing his spiritual responsibilities. The appendix includes some informal essays addressing several aspects or issues students say are especially challenging. These include how to communicate a vision, the centrality and requirements of honesty and trust, how to delegate, the relevance of loyalty in today's business world, and when a person should quit his position.

Questions for Discussion:

1. How do you define *effective leadership*? Explain how it is an art or a science or both.
2. Consider the leaders for whom you have worked. Were they effective as leaders? Were they ethical? Which of their leadership approaches and behaviors do you desire to adopt (or avoid) in your own practice as a leader?
3. Would you prefer to work for an effective non-Christian or an ineffective Christian leader? Explain your answer.
4. Is the true leader of a group or organization always the person appointed to the leadership position? If not, how should the followers relate to the appointed leader?
5. How should a leader promote consensual commitment to the organizational purpose and goals among other members of the organization?
6. Can people be taught to be good leaders? Why or why not? What can you do to become more teachable?

CHAPTER 3

SPIRITUAL LEADERSHIP

"And as for me, this is my covenant with them," says the LORD:
"My Spirit which is upon you, and my words which I have put
in your mouth, shall not depart from your mouth, nor from the
mouth of your offspring's offspring," says the LORD, "from
now and forever."—Isaiah 59:21

Well-known British business author Charles Handy (1999) has called for individuals and organizations to find purpose for their journeys rather than focusing on money and profits. Although no widespread consensus has emerged as to the appropriate nature of spirituality or as to "the how" of integrating it with ethical concerns, a general interest in spirituality has grown in recent years. A growing number of organizations sponsor workshops, seminars, retreats, and spiritual exercises to help employees examine themselves emotionally and spiritually. There is a movement within not-for-profit and for-profit sectors to incorporate ethical principles and practices pertaining to issues of transparency, diversity, transcultural dynamics, sustainability, the environment, and human development. Large corporations, think tanks, and political leaders increasingly rely on spirituality as a form of human resource development. Companies hope this will produce more psychologically content employees who will be productive and enthusiastic about their work.

Spirituality can be viewed in various ways. The introduction to this volume notes that spirituality can be conceived broadly as encompassing the aspects of the individual's search for inner peace and serenity; personal integrity and transparency including respect, trust, forgiveness, and love in our relationships; one's concern for social justice and environmental stewardship; and one's vision for the world and sense of personal calling in life (Dorr 2008). Mitroff and Denton (1999) define spirituality as "the basic feeling of being connected with one's complete self, others, and the entire universe."

From an open worldview perspective, spirituality involves recognizing the reality and value of influences beyond the closed material universe. Whereas some consider spirituality to be a religious concern, others view it as secular or without a need to relate it to any religious persuasion. Archie Carroll (2009, 162) writes that those searching for a secular spirituality seek a deeper and more meaningful understanding of why they are here, why they are in their particular workplace positions, and what the future holds. A secular individual accepts the existence of something larger than himself or herself, but does not rely on any specific religious belief system in searching for interconnectedness. A religious spirituality also demands that leaders cultivate and nourish a sense of self that recognizes the interrelatedness of life or a sense of community (Fluker 2008).

This is the understanding depicted in Charles Dickens's well-known and beloved *A Christmas Carol* (1843). Despicable Ebenezer Scrooge is introduced as a selfish, money-grubbing business owner existing in a closed, materialist, and small world. His hardened disbelief and denial of spiritual concerns is eventually overcome after a series of terrifying visits and dire warnings from the ghost of his deceased former partner Jacob Marley and the ghosts of Christmas Past, Christmas Present, and Christmas Yet to Come. These spirits show him his true self through depictions of his own Christmases and their consequences. Desperate, he comes to repent. Even he had a spark of inner spirit, though extremely dimmed, that was revived and burst forth as he became a person who exemplified the spirit of Christmas, a man of generosity and goodwill who relearned how to love others, especially Tiny Tim. Formerly lonely and miserable, Scrooge was changed into a joyful and happy man, a man of open-system spirituality. He even became a reasonable, generous spiritual leader in his business.

The recent increase in attention to spirituality in business possibly stems from a greater demand by people for meaning and purpose in their work. In Mitroff and Denton's (1999) spiritual audit of working people, respondents most often agree that workplace meaning and purpose come from

- realizing one's full potential as a person;
- being associated with a good organization or ethical organization;
- interesting work;
- making money;
- having good colleagues; serving humankind;
- servicing future generations; and
- servicing immediate communities.

Leaders who recognize the importance of spirituality and who recognize a holistic responsibility for others, particularly their followers or clients, need to develop practical ways for offering them meaning and purpose. This can be a challenging objective in the prevailing culture, one suggesting the need for some paradigm shifts in viewing leadership responsibilities. Indeed, action-oriented leaders often consider contemplation of philosophic presuppositions to be an academic diversion, if they consider them at all. Leaders on the firing line, whether they are business executives, college presidents or deans, service professionals, or middle managers, are responsible for making decisions and seeing that their organizations implement them effectively and efficiently. Pragmatism is sometimes considered a practical virtue enabling decisiveness, even if this leads to subordinating means to ends and neglecting spiritual ends for financial goals.

For example, a college dean might cancel low-enrolled (though still incrementally profitable) courses to improve the ratios upon which he is measured, although students who were relying on these courses in their academic plans interpret the cancellations as promise breaking. The dean is possibly acting in the best interests of the institution, relying on a utilitarian logic according to generally accepted academic procedures. But how does this influence moldable students? Greater, more explicit attention to exemplifying a biblical or other spiritual worldview might not change the dean's or business manager's decision, but it may lead to his changing his manner of implementation and influence him to seek ways to ameliorate future unfairness or insensitivity. Would not a superior leader seek creative solutions that better satisfy both spiritual and financial needs?

Admittedly, the prevailing purposes, values, and practices of Western business leaders ignore or at least subordinate any spiritual influence (Dorr 2008); for example, they seek profitability as the ultimate "bottom line" as opposed to viewing it as an important (even commendable) means to more meaningful ends. Without a rich understanding of the moral and spiritual implications of what people do in their businesses, they misunderstand their contribution to the wider society and ultimately lose perspective of their very selves and their companies (Naughton and Cornwall 2009, 3). When leaders ignore the spiritual dimension, this diminishes them as leaders and persons who otherwise would search for meaning and the significance of the responsibilities that they have been given. There may be few as miserable as Scrooge, but each leader should consider the personal and social risks of a Nietzschean view that ethics, especially when presented as spiritually based, is really no more than a fictional means for gaining self-gratifying power over others.

A spiritual leader should not be controlled and determined by compulsions for workaholism or pragmatic reactions to please others, whether organizational superiors, peers, subordinates, or other stakeholders but instead should strive to be genuinely free to trust and follow that to which one is most profoundly called. This in no way means that a Christian spirituality is mechanical or irrational; the leader must apply her capacity for independent thought and action as she seeks to bridge any gap between her deeper, inner self and her ultimate source of calling, which for the Christian leader is the Triune God.

Spiritual leadership also can take many non-Christian forms (e.g., see Pruzan and Miller 2006; also see Hazony 2012, for an intriguing Jewish perspective). It often originates in the human, essentially man-centered rather than God-centered. Man-centered influences are numerous, ranging from New Age pantheisms to self-righteous, egoistic pragmatism. A Christian must carefully test the spiritual winds to avoid great peril (John 3:8; 2 Peter 2:20-22). The spiritual approach recommended in this book is Trinitarian, which seeks to conform to orthodox Christianity that maintains God is of one nature in three persons.

Special Characteristics of the Spiritual Leader

The successful spiritually minded leader, whether religious or not, is one who causes others to seek out and understand their inner selves and who fosters a sense of meaning and significance among his or her followers. He strives to encourage a sense of significance and interconnectedness among employees (Barnett 2010). Spiritual leadership involves the application of spiritual values and principles to the workplace. It is concerned with the development of employees as "whole people." Whereas there is little empirical evidence that any particular leadership approach or style is more or less consistent with spirituality in the workplace, Barnett (2010, 5) suggests the two leadership approaches of transformational leadership and servant leadership seem to be more closely related to the concept of spiritual leadership than others.

Regardless of worldview or religious persuasion, attention to spiritual leadership is often missing in the leader's pressured rush toward pragmatism. When he neglects to engage in soul-searching inquiry as to meaning and responsibility, the leader ultimately falls short by elevating financial profits to ends rather than understanding them as important means. Building one's character is far more important than having a manual for problem-solving (Murphy 2008, 126). A leader should develop the moral character as well as the technical skills to inspire others toward a meaningful purpose. Ronald Reagan preferred to describe himself as a "communicator of great things" rather than the "great communicator."

While people in any culture still search for a firm footing, self-development, and the confirmation of others, they have become increasingly dependent on the praise they receive in the work arena. To satisfy their perceived need for confirmation, many are prepared to do virtually anything, even sacrifice quality of life and good health to serve the company credo, its moral code, and its cultural rites. Indeed, an organization's human resource policies can seek to manipulate the desires, fears, and imaginations—and thus the souls—of its employees (Verstraeten 2008). Such companies behave like pseudo-religions and in some instances do not even hesitate to manipulate the desire for immortality (Aubert 1996; Verstraeten 2008, 137).

Institutions and professional environments often function under the illusion that they are divine and all-powerful institutions (Aubert 1996).

The relationship of dependence in the work environment is especially noticeable and sometimes tragic when the organization restructures through downsizing; individuals finding meaning in their organization can fall into an existential vacuum of despair when their ties are severed. Instead, a person periodically needs to step away from his workplace to enjoy other activities or leisure for the renewal of a spiritual perspective and its confirmation (McCoy 2007), balancing his life according to the personal value: "My life does not belong to my job and my company."

According to Burkard Sievers (1996), Verstraeten (2008, 142) says one of the most pertinent deficiencies among top managers is the illusion that they enjoy imperishable power over others. The person guilty of self-deification, of turning himself or herself into God, is also likely to exhibit the tendency to subject others to himself or herself, to reify them and manipulate them (as parts of the machine to be manipulated as he so chooses). Silence and meditation can lead one to realize one's own mortality, that one exists among other mortal human creatures. Genuine leadership demands that one recognizes his own weaknesses and limitations; this will allow him to recognize the vulnerability of others and deal with them differently. One's leadership qualities and creativity can then be set free, so he or she can lead spiritually, and thus meaningfully.

It is critical thought that activates the moral imagination needed by leaders (Hartman 2008). This is a prime resource for leaders in finding innovative practical solutions as well as in transcending intellectual situations. Leaders must possess the attributes of action, courage, and experimentalism to find ways to escape from the comfort zones of established identity-based enclaves. For example, management practices for overcoming racism and sexism can be developed as leaders think through differences (e.g., what it means to be somebody else in circumstances other than their own).

Spiritual leadership requires courage of the will and some thickness of skin. Today's leader should not expect to be applauded any more than was the person who, after struggling out of the cave and returning to free others in Plato's *The Republic*, was then killed by those he freed. Perhaps today's leader can apply moral imagination creatively to seek and promote a creative alternative solution that furthers the organizational agenda and the desired ends of stakeholders. However, seeking to lead by challenging closed conceptual frameworks, opening the path to different meanings, and introducing new visions is not always politically correct. The wise leader must pick his battles carefully, but a spiritually-minded leader often must courageously demonstrate willpower. He must be willing to die for something (Solzhenitsyn 1978) or at least to put calling before social acceptance and, at times, job security. If not, is he a genuine leader?

General Robert E. Lee, shortly after his total defeat in 1865, exemplified such spiritual leadership. During a service at St. Paul's Episcopal Church in Richmond, where many prominent Confederate leaders worshipped, a black man rose to accept communion. According to an eyewitness, "the effect on those present was startling, and for several moments they retained their seats in solemn silence and did not move" and the priest was "embarrassed." But Lee went forward and knelt beside the black man at the chancel rail. The other communicants followed, and the peace of St. Paul's was restored (Crocker 1999). Robert E. Lee manifested the character and genuine spirituality to lead others to overcome social, cultural, and situational walls, demonstrating he genuinely lived according to his motto *vincit qui se vincit* ("he conquers who conquers himself").

But too few manifest the leadership character of Lee. Despite the increase in research, writing, and teaching of business ethics in universities worldwide, especially over the past thirty years, has the overall ethical standing of business improved, at least as perceived by members of the global society? This question itself deserves research. Perhaps business graduates and practitioners in some industries and regions can be shown to be better informed as to the ethical aspects of situations, certainly in environmental and certain human rights areas such as discrimination and tolerance. Business ethics courses also generally seek to enhance students' proficiency in ethical analysis. However, Stark's (1993) controversial claim, basically that business ethics is failing in the eyes of businesspeople, still has a ring of truth. Indeed, the *Wall Street Journal* daily reports new scandals and failures of corporate leaders, Wall Street financiers, and government officials. Perhaps such continuing corruption has a spiritual source. If the appropriate purpose of business ethics is to promote the ethical enhancement of business practice, as well as to raise ethical sensitivity and provide analytical competence, and if such practice is indeed subject to influence from a spiritual dimension, then a spiritual recognition may lead to more complete understanding of the real problem. This is at least the hope of those who seek to consider the role of spirituality in ethical leadership.

Perhaps the reader is by now somewhat convinced of the value of leading with an openness to spiritual concerns. But she also needs to know what these spiritual concerns are and how they can be incorporated by a leader. The previous discussion has referred to some of these, but only in a general and incomplete manner. This Christian author cannot offer definitive, universal answers, ones that would appropriately satisfy leaders of all spiritual persuasions and worldviews. Instead, part III seeks to explore leadership ethics and spirituality in greater depth by restricting the discussion to that of Christian spirituality. The following chapters address the attributes that can equip a Christian to develop as a good leader, one who can lead effectively, ethically, and with spiritual-mindedness.

Questions for Discussion:

1. If business is or should be more than maximizing profits, does this mean it involves spiritual purposes as well as material ones? What does it mean to be successful in business from a spiritual perspective?

2. Is it ethically justified for a leader to seek to influence the spiritual beliefs of those she leads in the workplace? If so, does this make it okay to try to convert subordinates or fellow workers if your employer establishes a policy against this?

3. In what other ways should a Christian (or a follower of another faith) offer spiritual leadership on the job?

4. What do you see are the benefits, if any, of leading with an openness to spiritual concerns? What are the possible pitfalls?

PART III

THE ATTRIBUTES OF A
GOOD CHRISTIAN LEADER

A Christian leader is called by God as a Christian and also as a leader. To be a good leader, a person must learn to progress in effectiveness as a technically competent leader. As a Christian, a leader also needs to grow in his spiritual understanding according to a biblically-based worldview and in his ability to apply a sound Christian ethic in the workplace.

The following chapters address five attributes that a Christian should develop to promote her growth as an effective, ethical, and spiritually minded leader. These attributes are not quantifiable, but together comprise a qualitative model. They do not offer the specificity of a cookbook or mathematical formula, but do outline basic guideposts a Christian can use as starting points for self-assessment.

The five attributes of a good Christian leader are:

1. *He must be called as a Christian,* justified by faith in Jesus Christ.
2. *He must be called as a leader,* accepting the responsibility for seeing that followers strive together for a collective purpose.
3. *He should develop and consistently apply a biblical worldview.*
4. *He must practice his leadership in conformance with a sound Christian ethic.*
5. *He should practice his leadership, including his style, behavioral approaches, and decisions in an excellent manner.* He must competently apply technical principles, styles, and models of leadership and apply them ethically and spiritually.

CHAPTER 4

A DOUBLE CALLING

And when He had spoken this, He said to him, "Follow me!"—
John 21:19b

A spiritually minded leader seeks to bridge the gap between her deeper, inner self and her ultimate source of calling. For a professing Christian to be a good leader, he or she must be called as a righteous believer in Jesus Christ *and* as a responsible leader in a leadership role. Two distinct divine callings are required (attributes #1 and #2). This chapter discusses the basis and nature of this double calling.

Whether or not a person is a Christian, he or she can serve as a good (effective, ethical, and spiritually minded) leader, one who responsibly organizes his followers to strive together for a collective purpose. Leadership effectiveness is expressed through behaviors that one learns through God's common grace, which He provides to all people. This includes knowledge gained through tacit experience and study.

Christians are those God calls to repentance and faith in Jesus Christ, independent of their occupational role. A Christian is not automatically a good leader nor superior to all non-believers in terms of effectiveness in leading others. Nevertheless, every Christian, saved by grace, can think of himself as a full-time Christian worker, for he is created in Christ Jesus for good works (Ephesians 2:8-10). How does his becoming a new spirit-filled creation impact his professional working career or occupation?

When counseling enthusiastic new converts who desire to serve God, pastors often encourage them to attend seminary. There they will receive professional education equipping and pointing them to the pastoral ministry or other religious occupations such as the mission field, church education, or Christian counseling. This may well be commendable, but does genuine conversion, along with a heartfelt desire to grow in the knowledge and service of Christ, always mean that a person should enter a religious occupation?

Indeed, is "full-time Christian work" as a preacher, missionary, or church administrator always a higher calling than to a secular vocation? Not according to Puritans such as William Perkins (n.d.). They had a more expansive view, speaking of the two parts of God's calling—(1) the general call to faith (2 Thessalonians 2:14, Acts 16:31); and (2) one's particular call to vocation (1 Corinthians 7:20). A person's highest vocational calling may be to the pastoral ministry *or* it may be to another occupation. Numerous testimonies of successful leaders support this position.

Personal Testimonies of Leaders

John Calvin, the great leader of the Reformation, was asked by Guillaume Farel in 1536 to stay in Geneva to help build the church there. But Calvin refused, explaining that he was a scholar and not a minister. Calvin, however, experienced a burden that was not relieved until he took the church assignment in Geneva for the remainder of his life. Calvin wrote Farel, "No lessor tie would have been sufficient to retain me there so long, had it not been that I dared not throw off the yoke of my calling, which I was well assured had been laid on me by God" (John Calvin, *Letters*, 1:213).

Sam Walton, founder of Walmart, wrote of his being called to discount retailing:

> Having thought about this a lot, I can honestly say that if I had the choices to make all over again, I would make just about the same ones. Preachers are put here to minister to our souls; doctors to heal our diseases; teachers to open up our minds; and so on. Everybody has their role to play. The thing is, I am absolutely convinced

that the only way we can improve one another's quality of life, which is something very real to those of us who grew up in the Depression, is through what we call free enterprise—practiced correctly and morally. (Walton 1992, 252)

Nicholas Wolterstorff writes that he is called to academics: "The work of a professor is something to which some of us are called by God—in the classic sense of Luther and Calvin, such that if we did not do it, we would be acting disobediently. I think I have been called to be a professor of philosophy. Although I love carpentry and am—I think—good at it, I think I would be disobedient if I took that up as a profession. I and all of us are called to do other things" (Wolterstorff 1992, 19).

John Templeton was called to be a financial investor. Michael Novak (1996) writes that when Templeton was a boy growing up in Tennessee, he had wanted to be a missionary. But while studying at Yale and Oxford, he met a number of Christian missionaries home from the field and recognized that he did not have the right stuff, that others had much more talent as missionaries than he did. But he also recognized that he was more talented with money, so he devoted himself to helping the missionaries financially.

These are only four of many examples of such testimonies (see Novak 1996 for others). Such empirical evidence does not prove but certainly gives credence to the Puritans' concept of God's double calling: to repentance, faith, and obedience, and also to occupation.

Is the Concept of Double Calling Correct?

However, many Christian scholars (e.g., Harkness 1931; Coenen 1975; Chewning, Eby, and Roels 1990), to varying degrees, qualify or broaden the Puritan concept of a person's vocation to include family and social responsibilities as well as his workplace occupation or role. This more general interpretation softens Paul's exhortation and allows Harkness (1931, 213) to claim that even John Calvin (*Letters*, 1:213) does not equate a man's vocation with his means of livelihood. But when Paul said, "Let each man remain in that condition in which he was called," was Paul not referring to a specific call to a specific occupation? Although he used the Greek *kaleo* or *klesis* with this meaning in no place other than 1 Corinthians 7:20, he could very well use the same word in more than one sense. Recognizing this, and interpreting the verse within the context of what Paul was saying in the surrounding passage, supports the interpretation of the Reformers and Puritans (Hodge 1857, 122-23; also see Whetstone 1991, 173-77). When God calls a person to repentance and faith, a new spiritual and moral state, He may well approve of the redeemed person remaining in his previous vocation in the world, whether it is in the marketplace, the academy, the home, or somewhere else as a steward of God's creation. Paul thus did not urge every new convert to leave his job or station and become a full-time Christian worker, although he needed many new laborers to help him build the church. He instead wrote that believers should stick to their business, to work quietly, and to eat their own bread, which they earn through work (e.g., 1 Thessalonians 4:11, 12; 2 Thessalonians 3:10, 12). A convert may sense a call to the professional ministry, but choosing this or any new occupation is a serious commitment; abandoning one's vocational calling may risk leaving God's will.

Martin Luther led the way toward the Puritans' expansive concept of dual calling, focusing on the Christian's responsibility of service in the world. Every Christian has a God-given vocation that should serve as a station from which to serve others. John Calvin (1960) agreed, teaching that God has appointed duties for every man in his particular way of life. This means that each Christian should be grateful for the opportunity for service and should prepare for the positions for which he or she is best qualified (Heiges 1984). Meeting this responsibility leads to great blessing; contentment in life is largely a function of abiding in one's calling because this is consistent with God's will.

The Reformers' view of calling is a long way from the classical Greek belief that manual work is of lower value than intellectual pursuits, even demeaning. Although the worthiness of work, including manual labor, is a central teaching of the *Rule of St. Benedict*, for centuries the standard guide for monastic life in the West (Hill 1990), medieval Catholicism had a view of divine calling applying only to the religious life, distinguishing the sacred and secular. The Reformers, with their doctrines of justification by faith alone and the priesthood of all believers, broke down such secular versus sacred barriers. A shepherd watching his flock is in as honorable a vocation as is a magistrate ruling over his constituents or as a preacher preaching (Perkins n.d.). Agreeing with the Reformers and Puritans, Roman Catholic priest Robert Sirico (2001) says businesspeople, including entrepreneurs and leaders in all varieties of organizations, are indeed called to their occupational role. The calling is from God; it helps one to affirm the dignity of the enterprise one undertakes, and it comes with certain moral responsibilities (e.g., note Luke 19:11-27). Each Christian is to search out the proper works of his calling and to do them. The testimonies of Calvin, Walton, Wolterstorff, and Templeton support this view of calling—that it applies to business and economics and other God-ordained careers as well as to the gospel ministry.

A New Testament Perspective—The Parable of the Talents

The Gospels record that Jesus was very interested in how people worked in the economic and business realms of life. In many of his parables, Jesus describes the occupational practices of farmers, merchants, investors, fishermen, and housewives (e.g., Matthew 13). For example, in the Parable of the Talents (Matthew 25:14-30), Jesus offers lessons about the proper use of capital, investment, entrepreneurship, and economic resources, even though his main lesson is about discipleship. This parable does not condemn but honors proper risk-taking and entrepreneurship. God does not assign specific activities for multiplying the talents He gives; He does not state a set return-on-investment goal. Nevertheless, He expects, without having to say it, that a servant will endeavor to be creative in such investment and will not be adverse to risk losing it, if done so in the sincere process of seeking an increase beneficial to the Master. This is a direct rebuttal to those who insist that business success and Christian living are contradictory (Sirico 2001, 23). Indeed, it is moral rather than immoral to profit from creative, adventuresome application of one's God-given resources, wit, and labor. This is what the Christian is called to do in the workplace. Moreover, the religious community should not condemn those gifted for business, stock trading, or investment banking (Sirico 2001, 8) but encourage and support them in entrepreneurial business callings.

The risk-adverse, worthless servant is the key to this lesson from this parable. A servant's success or failure is not measured solely in terms of quantitative output but primarily in terms of heart attitude. The servant who made two talents and the servant who made five are both honored. The servant declared "worthless" would have been honored if he had merely made the standard rate of interest, but he was dishonored because he hid the talent to prevent its theft. "Playing it safe" is not the best option nor really a safe one for the person who truly knows his Master. Instead, Christians are to confront uncertainty as to how to apply their talents in imaginative, creative ways, using what Patricia Werhane (1999) calls *moral imagination*.

Discovering One's Calling

Robert Novak (1996) identifies four characteristics of one's calling: (1) it is unique to the individual; (2) it has certain preconditions, such as one having the right talents, skills, and personality; (3) the individual finds it enjoyable and fulfilling, in spite of any drudgery or frustrations involved; and (4) discovering one's calling is often not easy. Seeking God's calling is a duty for the Christian, even if it proves difficult.

British minister Alan Redpath (1954) helpfully addressed the individual's challenge of finding his vocational calling with the following story. A ship approached a coastal port in dense fog. Even though the night was dark and the fog obscured visibility, the ship's captain confidently shouted the command to turn into the harbor, and the ship entered the narrow channel between rocky reefs. A passenger, puzzled and impressed as to how the captain knew when to turn the ship, asked for an explanation. The captain responded that he merely looked for three red lights, barely visible through the fog. One was at the mouth of the channel, one was at the dock, and one was in between, on a buoy in the channel. When the three lights were aligned, the captain knew to order the ship to turn safely into port. Analogously, the following three lights are signposts for choosing one's calling:

- Follow the precepts of Scripture.
- Follow the inward witness of the Holy Spirit.
- Follow outward circumstances.

When all three are aligned, a person may safely proceed with the assurance of being in God's will.

Practical in their spirituality, Puritans such as Perkins advised each person to examine himself or herself concerning what he or she is most apt or fit to do. For this, the person can weigh his own greatest interests and gifts, the observation and advice of parents or other trusted counselors, and the outward calling, including recruitment, by other people. Gift assessment and career counseling are important helps if used as a supplement to the inward leading of the Holy Spirit as prayerfully interpreted according to Scripture (Proverbs 11:14, 29:18).

Called to be a Leader

God's cultural mandate commissions every human person to cultivate the earth and rule over other creatures (Genesis 1:28, 2:15, 3:23). Chapter 2 describes leadership as a function in which a person with the right skills renders a service for the whole group by moving others to accomplish a purpose. Within a social organization or group, a person can be designated with an occupational role as a leader. But does God call particular persons to be leaders?

Legitimate leadership is an occupational role in the natural sphere. Moreover, social scientists say everyone has potential to lead (Wefald and Katz 2007), and that everyone can develop leadership skills (Krueger 2007), although experts differ as to whether all have the same potential to lead. Lussier and Achua (2010) observe that some people are blessed with more innate leadership ability than others. Furthermore, some men and women willfully aspire to lead or have greater opportunities to lead others in formal or informal roles. Other individuals are less willing to take on at least some leadership roles, seeming to prefer being followers in their particular situational contexts or social organizations.

A Christian worldview, recognizing the spiritual reality of God's concerned intervention into the natural realm, adds depth to the above observations. According to an open-system worldview perspective, God providentially upholds, directs, disposes, and governs all creatures, actions, and things, ordinarily through the secondary means in the natural sphere (Westminster Confession of Faith, 1:1, 3). Since leaders and their organizational roles are within God's governance, it is most reasonable to hold that God does issue a spiritual call to some persons to carry out a leadership role as his primary vocational occupation, while not calling others. A person can sense a calling to leadership when he is legitimately appointed or recruited by a group or organization, when he has followers, and when he has a personal desire to accept leadership responsibilities. Of course some people in their free wills take on leadership roles or are appointed to formal leadership roles to which they may not be truly called. Others may not respond to a calling to lead. Nor does everyone recognize or respond to his true calling. It is thus important for a Christian asked to assume a leadership role to seek to confirm his sense of calling to that particular leadership role—as to any occupational role— through both natural and spiritual self-assessment. Assurance of being in the right calling is a blessing; each spiritually minded person should consider his sense of calling through scriptural meditation and prayer, thereby seeking to confirm his being in God's will. This is an important aspect of his spiritual obligations, to God, and to his fellow men and women.

A Person's Calling Can Change

Whatever the person's calling, to leave it means taking a downward (suboptimal) course because he then neglects the priorities God has set (Gariepy 1991; note Nehemiah 6:3). It is thus not usually advisable to "job hop." Nevertheless, a person's vocational calling can change. If an individual grows restless on the job, considering a change might be consistent with God's will. Two Old Testament leaders exemplify this: Nehemiah did move on after the wall was built, and Caleb, at the age of eighty-five, took the challenge to drive the fearsome Anakim from Hebron.

Summary

A Christian who is rightly serving as a leader is dually called to be both a righteous believer and an effective leader (an overlap or conjunction of the spiritual and natural world spheres). Seeking God's calling to vocation in the material world is a spiritual duty for the Christian, even though this challenge can prove difficult. The Holy Spirit will guide the seeker who earnestly prays and draws on scriptural confirmation of his desires, gifts, and opportunities. A person in his right calling—whether to the ministry, business, the law, medicine, manual labor, or academics—will possess a certain basic contentment, in spite of weariness and frustration from time to time. The Christian is wise to resist leaving his calling, but his calling can change during his working lifetime. God may use restlessness or discontentment to motivate him to consider a change.

Regardless of age or situation, a Christian should apply a sound ethic from a biblical worldview as she works in her calling, whether as a leader or a follower. The next several chapters more fully explain how a Christian who recognizes her calling to a responsible leadership position applies worldview thinking (chapter 5) and ethical analysis (chapters 6 and 7) as she seeks to fulfill her double calling.

Questions for Discussion:

1. Do you know a non-Christian whom you consider to be a good leader? What makes him or her a good leader?
2. Do you know any professing Christians whom you consider to be poor leaders? What skills, behavioral practices, or character qualities do they lack? Do you lack any of these, as well? Do you see some ways to avoid such negatives in order to improve yourself as a leader?
3. Are you working in the position or job where you believe God has called you? What makes you think so? If not, are you willing to seek out a job in your proper calling? What will it take for you to achieve this?
4. Are leaders most basically born to leadership or are they made?
5. If you are recruited or promoted to a leadership role at work, what should you consider carefully before accepting it?

CHAPTER 5

WORLDVIEW

Finally, brethren, whatever is true, whatever is honorable,
whatever is right, whatever is pure, whatever is lovely, whatever
is of good repute, if there is any excellence and if anything
worthy of praise, let your mind dwell on these things.—
Philippians 4:8

A spiritually minded leader thinks and acts according to his or her worldview, which is a way of thinking about the world. A worldview is not a philosophy, theology, or system of thought but a perceptual framework. A person's values, what he most wants to occur, are based on his basic worldview presuppositions.

Everyone has a worldview, although some may not realize this. A person's worldview is significantly influenced by his culture, which in turn is generally rooted in a dominant worldview. It will influence how he lives and even how he dies. People with differing worldviews may have difficulty communicating or understanding one another because they have differences in their perception of reality.

Alben Barkley, vice president under Truman, when delivering the keynote address in Lexington, Virginia, at the 1956 Washington and Lee Mock Convention, offered his worldview: "I would rather be a doorkeeper in the house of my God than to dwell in the tents of wickedness" (Psalm 84:10b). Immediately following this pronouncement, he fell dead at the podium. Confusion broke out at the mock convention, but Vice President

Barkley ended his life journey with a proclamation of his worldview that honorably testified to his leadership.

How to Develop as a Worldview Thinker

As an important part of his education, a Christian should deliberately seek to understand his basic presuppositions according to a spiritually engaged open-system worldview. Exhibit 2 provides an example. Worldview thinking is essential for a Christian called to a leadership role. He can apply his worldview understanding as he learns to address world realities in a variety of ways, applying empiricism, reason, intuition, and faith (Curtis 2000).

Cognitive worldview knowledge is found in Scripture, in sermons, and in publications of worldview scholars (e.g., Kuyper 1931; Wolterstorff 1976; Blamires 1978; Holmes 1983; Walsh and Middleton 1984; Chewning 1989; Sire 1997; Plantinga 2002), as well as in any literature that reveals truths about creation realities. A person requires such cognitive knowledge for discernment, for making decisions, and for articulating viewpoints stemming from a worldview. Tacit knowledge is required as well, including that from sources such as experience and nonverbal lessons from living, doing, striving, and receiving information.

A prospective leader can develop his own worldview by observing good leaders and by listening to and absorbing the wise counsel of personal mentors. The latter is especially common in some cultures, such as Asian ones (see Yutang 1931), where elders are honored. However, in some cultures, and increasingly in the West, seniors are often disparaged as being no longer in touch. But the following account suggests that an elderly person can serve a vital worldview-anchoring role in Western cultures as well, a lesson that prospective leaders ignore at their and their culture's peril.

Dr. John Reed Miller was a man of God who helped form and reinforce a Christian worldview in many of his disciples. After a long career as a Presbyterian minister, college president, and leader of other pastors, he spent his retirement years primarily in Bible study, prayer, and mentoring young pastors and seminary students. Dr. Miller met with a mentee almost every day of his retirement, usually while dining at his favorite restaurant. In his last years, he lost his eyesight and his overall health, forcing him to move to a nursing home. Though no longer able to go to restaurants, he continued to mentor from his bed. One day a visitor told him of her recent business luncheon at one of the casinos in a nearby river town. Dr. Miller was shocked upon learning of the introduction of legalized gambling in our state. Still committed to his calling as a leader, Dr. Miller prayed as to what he could do. Several days later, he dictated the following:

> God's Providence is His most wise and powerful governing of all creatures in all their needs. Gambling, on the other hand, assumes the rightness of fate, chance, and luck. These are pagan ideas. They oppose the true God and His Providence at every turn. A Christian should not play with such evil. (Miller n.d.)

Dr. Miller asked his visitor to print copies of his statement on cards for distribution to Christian friends and others. Even while he was totally physically disabled and past usefulness in the eyes of most, this man's character, built upon coherent, consistent, and open worldview convictions, led him to do what he could to oppose the social malady of gambling. Drawing upon his worldview, he led as he believed Christ compelled him until the very end of his days.

Worldview thinking is not merely a passive, academic endeavor; it influences beliefs that lead to changing the world. In fifth-century Rome, a Christian monk named Telemachus leaped into the gladiatorial arena to stop the combatants. As he repeatedly pleaded, "In the name of God, stop!" the mob stoned him to death for interfering with the combat they valued as entertainment. The Emperor thereupon ordered that the bloody spectacles be stopped and Telemachus be enrolled among the martyrs. According to LaTourette (1975), economic and social forces, specifically the growing poverty in the declining Roman Empire and a lack of recruits for the gladiatorial ranks contributed to the end of the contests in the arena between men and beasts as much as did the appeal to Christian conscience. Nevertheless, Telemachus's bold action was the catalyst that highlighted the moral need for the ban. His sacrificial protest, not tolerant or politically correct if viewed through a postmodern lens, was a courageous demonstration of the moral application of Christian worldview thinking.

A Christian worldview recognizes that everyone has a fallen nature. Christians cannot claim to have greater technological or intellectual competency than non-Christians (Chewning et al. 1990, 47), nor are they any more worthy of God's grace. Because leaders may have to place people in situations involving temptation, they are thus responsible for providing controls on those temptations, for rewarding people for avoiding temptations, and for creating environments that minimize the susceptibility to temptations. Nevertheless, the leader must still respect the inherent worth of every other human creature, for everyone bears God's image (see exhibit 2). Pope John Paul II's philosophy joins with that of the Reformers in that all human creatures are worthy of dignity and respect (Wojtyla 1981). This is a basic starting point for a Christian ethic. Without this presupposition, a person's ethic is corrupt at its foundation; but if it is incorporated into the person's worldview, he can develop into a man of integrity.

Leaders Need to Recognize Worldview Differences

A leader needs to subscribe to a sound worldview, one that is open, comprehensive of all reality, and internally coherent (Walsh and Middleton 1984). He should also recognize the worldview of his followers. How can he lead well if he misunderstands his followers' basic worldviews?

A leader thus needs at least a basic understanding of alternative worldviews. He should especially study those prevalent among his employees and organizational context. Exhibit 3, "Modernism," and exhibit 4, "Postmodernism," describe two worldviews that are likely to influence employees in developed countries, although there are many variations and other religious views, such as animism, Taoism, and Islam, a leader might well encounter. The leader needs to know whether those he seeks to lead have a high or low opinion of human reason and logical analysis, if they believe that some truths are absolute or that truth and reality are socially constructed, if they believe human progress is inevitable or illusionary, if they view the human person as exalted or ultimately insignificant, if they believe in God or not, and if they trust that ethics and basic morality are created by God or by society or are nonexistent. Exhibit 5 offers a comparison of some presuppositions of Christianity, modernism, and postmodernism.

Leadership and Worldview Thinking

Although he should not expect to impose a complete set of worldview presuppositions upon another, a leader can help others understand and mold their worldviews. He may not have a formula or set pattern of procedures for doing this because it is more in the realm of art than science. But, as in promoting character development, the leader can influence others through his example, mentoring, and challenging assignments. The following personal anecdote illustrates this.

When I was a boy, I often begged my father to take me with him on his errands. Once, when I was five years old, he took me downtown where he had some business to conduct in our segregated Deep South town. So that I would not be a hindrance, he decided to leave me with a friend who worked, selling pencils and candy, at the intersection of the two main streets. I was surprised that this friend was a Black man who had no legs. He rested himself on a plank of wood that was set up on roller skates, somewhat like a skateboard. He maneuvered by pushing the board with his hands. This man was kind to me; he watched me play and we talked. I quickly came to like this man, who was my father's good friend. After about an hour, my father returned and took me home. Since then, I have wondered why my father left me with that particular man. My father died when I was eight so I cannot ask him why, but I believe he was trying to teach me a worldview lesson. Even as a child I realized the legless beggar was a good man. My father obviously trusted, respected, and liked this man for who he was, even though he had no social, economic, or educational attainments. Over time I came to realize he was worthy of my unqualified respect, since he was a man created in God's own image. This must be the lesson my father meant to teach me, helping me form a worldview understanding that I should apply to every person I encounter throughout life.

A person can continue to develop and refine his worldview throughout his life. Early experiences are extremely important. Parents naturally have great opportunity and responsibility for molding worldview presuppositions and basic beliefs of their children. A person is blessed when he is taught well by his parents and other early influencers, and even more blessed when he eventually understands the source of his world and life view.

A leader, whether a parent or a work supervisor, influences the basic worldview and values of those he encounters, whether he intentionally does so or not. It is incumbent on every leader to take care to set a positive example and offer morally sound lessons like the one my father taught me. Acting otherwise, based on my subsequent experience with my son, will almost definitely lead to others mimicking negative behaviors and habits that can even distort worldview thinking. For example, referring derogatively to members of a particular ethnic group can bias a person's understanding, values, and treatment of that group.

The leader also needs to acknowledge the law of unintended consequences, a phenomenon ignored with great risk. George Will (2010) comments on the consequences arising from the good intentions of the Anti-Saloon League and other American prohibitionists, prominently including women leaders such as Carry Nation, after they succeeded in securing passage of the Eighteenth Amendment to the US Constitution to outlaw the distribution and sale of alcoholic beverages. Evangelist Billy Sunday, preaching to ten thousand celebrants on January 16, 1920, enthusiastically proclaimed, "The reign of tears is over. The slums will soon be only a memory."

But the prohibition movement failed because it could not change human nature; it rested on a faulty worldview. Indeed, Prohibition led to establishment of a nationwide crime syndicate, the income tax (needed to replace lost federal alcohol tax revenues), plea bargaining, and a redefined role for the federal government and a privacy right—which eventually led to abortion rights (Okrent 2010). Prohibition was repealed after thirteen years, but the unintended consequences permanently changed America. Thoughtful Christian leaders need to apply much more moral imagination grounded in sound worldview consideration, going beyond mere linear thinking when backing social and institutional change. Effectiveness in lobbying and effecting simplistic bans is not the same as good leadership. Organizational administrators need to consider potential second-order and third-order implications of directives they issue to confront an emergent problem, which often can be an effect of a deeper, complex history of issues that may merely fester and perhaps grow more serious.

While essential, worldview knowledge nevertheless is not the entirety of knowledge, nor is it of much practical value to the leader unless he learns how to apply it appropriately in his role. This can be a difficult challenge amid the pressures and temptations faced by a leader in the complex reality of the fallen world. Successful engagement of this challenge involves ethical application of technical and biblical knowledge with spiritual discernment.

For example, leaders must be effective communicators. Good leaders say what they mean, but this does not excuse their choosing words without careful, empathetic consideration. Unfortunately, poor examples of "tone-deaf" statements abound among recognized leaders, and modern technology increasingly gives widespread exposure to leader gaffes. BP chairman Carl-Henric Svanberg has been reviled for saying, "We care about the small people." Actress Kristen Stewart offended rape survivors when she implied that the paparazzi cause her to feel raped when they take her photograph. Senator Harry Reid referred to President Obama as "light-skinned... with no Negro dialect." Michelle Obama said in a 2008 campaign rally, "For the first time in my adult lifetime, I am really proud of my country."

Sociological and cultural trends are not reassuring that such insensitivity is a temporary phenomenon while society adjusts to the information age. A University of Michigan study finds that empathy among college students has declined 40 percent over the past two decades (Zaslow 2010). Christians should not bow to this trend; instead, they should cultivate empathy in their leadership style. However, Scripture is clear that empathy is not to distort impartiality and justice in a dispute; a Christian should be biased neither toward the rich and powerful nor toward the poor (Exodus 23:2-3). A Christian leader consistently applying a biblical worldview needs to provide a positive, balanced example against this cultural trend, showing respect for other God-imagers through disciplined, just, and truly respectful communication.

Comprehensive, internally consistent, and open worldview thinking gives wise insights and value-based clarity to decisions that every leader needs to make. The next chapter discusses two of the many issues that a leader or follower is likely to face during her working career, the meaning of loyalty to a superior and the decision to develop a new product or service when co-workers oppose this. Note that these and indeed most decisions that leaders make have serious ethical implications. Thus, another requirement of a good, spiritually minded leader is to have and apply a sound ethic in her choices and behaviors. A Christian ethic is essential for making and actually implementing the practical decisions that her worldview will best support.

EXHIBIT 2
A CHRISTIAN WORLDVIEW

Our Relationship to God

God is infinite, eternal, omnipotent, omniscient, and holy. He created all things out of nothing and continues to guide all things by His sovereign providence. He created man (male and female) in His own image. God is both transcendent and immanent; He is the ruler of the universe and totally distinct from created beings, yet He enters into immediate fellowship with human creatures as the Triune God: Father, Son, and Holy Spirit. He has appointed people as His stewards over creation and requires worship and obedience to His moral law, which He established for the benefit of His creatures. God is loving and just. God commands us to love Him with all our hearts, souls, minds, and strength.

All humans are sinners against God, violating His commandments and justly deserving eternal punishment. But God is merciful and graciously provides eternal salvation and fellowship to those to whom He gives faith in Jesus Christ and His vicarious atonement. Each one God calls and regenerates as a born-again believer is continually sanctified by His word and the Holy Spirit dwelling within him, growing toward God's standard of holiness. This sanctification applies to the whole person, although it is imperfect in this life as the lusts of the flesh and corruption of the mind continue to war against the indwelling Spirit.

Our Relationship to Other People

Every human is a created being, always distinct from God the Creator, and limited in knowledge and power. People differ in character, talent, and skills, but all are equal before God in dignity and status. Because God created humans in His own image, people should always treat every person with dignity and respect. Every human sins, even regenerate Christians who are no longer slaves to sin. God commands people to love others, without approving of their sins.

EXHIBIT 2
A CHRISTIAN WORLDVIEW (CONTINUED)

Our Relationship to the World

People are to honor the world because it is God's creation. The fall has corrupted all created things, but His creation is still good. By His common grace, God sustains His creation and constrains the full effects of the fall, assigning and enabling humans to cultivate, rule, and advance civilization as His stewards.

EXHIBIT 3
MODERNISM
(CLOSELY TIED TO NATURALISM)

(1) Human reason is #1.

- o Humans can discover and communicate truth.
- o Science, technology, and economics ultimately provide all answers.
- o Tradition and history are not to be trusted—they have no purpose.

(2) Upward progress is inevitable.

- o Human understanding and society are always improving.
- o Old people and beliefs of former ages are out-of-date and generally inferior.

(3) The individual human person is exalted.

- o People are basically good.
- o People working together will make all things good.
- o People are complex biological and chemical beings—without soul or spirit.

(4) No transcendent God exists—or is irrelevant to progress.

- o The supernatural is a myth.
- o The cosmos exists as a closed system of cause and effect.
- o Death is the absolute end.

(5) Ethics and morals are created by humans in society.

- o Moral relativism prevails.
- o Standards change depending on the circumstances.
- o Environment determines behavior—men are not responsible but are victims.

EXHIBIT 4

POSTMODERNISM

(AFTER MODERNISM OR ANTI-MODERNISM)

(1) Truth and Reality are socially constructed.

o   There is no objective truth.

o   Reason is not meaningful; meaning is created by a social group and its language.

o   All communication is designed to oppress or manipulate others.

o   Hermeneutics of suspicion: every writing, every text is a political construction that must be deconstructed.

(2) Power prevails—might makes right.

o   Lies are okay if they work for me (and my group).

o   There are many cultures—the strongest wins out.

(3) The individual human person is not significant.

o   The self is dead.

o   A human person is worth no more than an insect ("A rat is a pig is a dog is a boy").

o   Nature and culture are exalted.

o   Image, style, and appearance matter more than a person's character.

o   Sensory gratification, entertainment, and promiscuity tend to be exalted.

o   People tend to drift, to become passive, insecure, cynical.

(4) God is dead.

(5) Morality does not exist—people act on impulse.

o   Uncritical tolerance is the only "value"—political correctness reigns.

o   "If God doesn't exist, all is possible."

EXHIBIT 5
A COMPARISON OF WORLDVIEW PRESUPPOSITIONS

	Biblical Christian	Modernism	Postmodernism
Truth	Revealed in Scripture and in the world; all truth is God's truth	Human reason is primary	No absolutes exist; truth and reality are socially constructed
Human Person	Created in God's image, a human is sinful but redeemable, spiritually and morally accountable, capable of and accountable for stewardship, and a developer of civilization	A material being and basically good	Insignificant with no meaningful purpose
God	Sovereign Creator, Redeemer, and Lord of all creation, transcendent and immanent	Irrelevant to progress in the natural world	God is dead
Source of Morality	The God of perfect character, love, and justice	Humans in society	Nonexistent or imposed by the powerful for their advantage

Questions for Discussion:

1. What is your personal worldview? A good exercise is to write down your basic views about God, how to relate to other people, and how to conduct yourself in the world. For this exercise it might help to think about what or who (parents, friends, teachers, pastors, coworkers, etc.) have been important influences as to what you most value and how you believe you should conduct your life.

2. In today's diverse, multi-cultural society, a leader must learn to work effectively with people with differing worldviews. How might you prepare for this reality, while remaining true to your own basic worldview values and beliefs?

3. Think of some people you work with or otherwise know well whose basic values and approaches to life seem to differ from yours. How might better understanding of your own worldview enable you to improve your relationships with them?

4. Can you recall a workplace situation where you felt right about making a decision or acting in ways that others thought were wrong? After reconsideration, do you still believe you were justified? Was the basic problem that your worldview clashed with the basic values and beliefs of the others? How might better communication have helped?

5. Is it ethical for a leader to try to influence followers to change their worldviews? If yes, does this mean you can use skills in psychological manipulation to "guilt" people in order to get them to change?

CHAPTER 6

ETHICAL ANALYSIS

A false balance is an abomination to the LORD, but a just weight is His delight.—Proverb 11:1

A Christian called to a leadership role is obligated to exercise his leadership responsibilities according to a sound ethic. This is of utmost importance. His behaviors and the policies and procedures he requires need to satisfy ethically justified standards distinguishing good versus bad, right versus wrong, and the virtuous versus vicious behavior. He must recognize that his ethical decisions can affect people as individuals, as members of institutions including his own, and throughout global society. Moreover, from an open-system perspective, he must continuously remain aware that ethical standards and decisions have spiritual dimensions due to the immanent influences and transcendent standards of God. This chapter starts by further discussing the nature of ethics, presents a practical decision model, and discusses some ethical criteria for guiding the analysis and implementation of ethical leadership.

Ethical Analysis Requires Study—Ethical Practice Also Requires More

Ethics is frequently defined as an academic discipline concerned with describing moral principles and values. *Webster's New Dictionary and Thesaurus* (1990) states that ethics is the study of standards of right and wrong or of a system of conduct and behavior or of moral principles. But in its practical application, ethics is not as dry as these definitions imply. Ethics can be complex, in practice if not in theory, because it involves the social interaction of humans. And practical ethical competence is essential for being a good leader.

Even when considered an academic subject, ethics is multidisciplinary. Philosophy and social science are both needed. Moral philosophy seeks to provide criteria and justification for a person's actions. Social science seeks to explain the influences on the person acting in a social context (Trevino 1986, 1990)—how and why we interrelate with others. Moreover, these disciplines should complement one another; Peter Winch (1958, 3) observes, "For any worthwhile study of society must be philosophical in character and any worthwhile philosophy must be concerned with the nature of human society."

But is academic study, even if interdisciplinary, sufficient for ethics? The answer perhaps would be yes—if the purpose of studying ethical behavior is to develop scientific, positive, and value-neutral descriptions of how humans behave. However, the subject matter of ethics involves values and morals; it encompasses more than merely describing how people actually behave. Whereas the sociologist asks, "Do Americans believe bribery is wrong?," the ethicist asks, "Is bribery wrong?" and "Why or why not?" Ethics, even as an academic subject, is concerned with developing adequate prescriptive claims or theories, whereas anthropological and sociological study of morality aims at being descriptive (Velasquez 1988, 11). Ethics is normative since it is used to determine standards of right and wrong human behavior; it focuses on "should" rather than just "is." Nevertheless, it must also be descriptive if it is to be grounded in actual human behavior in the context of actual situations; it must reflect a realistic understanding of what the world and human nature "are" to develop proper ideas of what they "should be."

Socrates is reputed to have said that ethics answers the basic human question, "How should one live?" Adapting this richer definition for an organizational leader, ethics can be viewed as how a leader should conduct himself in his role, on and off the job. More formally, an ethical leader not only must set forth a clear vision and purpose for followers but should honor the rights of others while fulfilling her own obligations in a principled manner (Whetstone 1997, 82).

Disciplined study is beneficial for ethics, but in practice the greatest human difficulty in ethical situations often is not to know the right action to take. Instead, it is actually undertaking that action. Ethics thus considers the character development of people, how they grow in terms of the moral qualities of character they need to dispose them actually to act appropriately (i.e., ethically).

This understanding suggests that the study of ethics should result in humans acting more ethically. Duska (1991, 331) says business ethics courses "can and should improve business behavior, and if they don't, there's not much point to them." This at least implies that a student of ethics should not only study the values and behaviors of humans, but he can also try to change his own behaviors and influence those of others. If ethics does indeed involve attempting to change people's moral character and values, as well as the way people behave, then ethics itself must be subjected to ethical analysis. A leader with influence over others should avoid unjustified interference (meddling).

Ultimately each decision maker must rely on his experience and practical judgment to decide how and to what extent to use his leadership influence. He should ground such judgments according to sound ethical standards in conformance with his worldview. For this, the spiritually minded leader should depend on scriptural guidance, counselors, and prayer to meet his ethical responsibilities.

The remainder of this chapter presents a basic decision model and discusses how it can be used to guide leaders in making and implementing ethical decisions. The next chapter then builds on the concepts introduced here in chapter 6, addressing how a worldview Christian can apply the basic decision outline in light of his spiritual awareness.

The Ethical Decision-Making Role of Leaders

Leaders are responsible for setting the vision for their organization and for choosing the strategies for moving people to identify with a common sense of direction. Their governing boards or owners, fellow leaders, and subordinates expect them to make effective and ethical decisions, as do governments, local and global communities, and, increasingly, environmental and other interest groups.

Clarity of worldview helps a person make timely decisions that consistently promote his deeply held values. It provides a basic grounding and guide for ethical decisions. In turn, a sound ethic can be instrumental for living and acting in accordance with his worldview. Ethics can be understood not merely as a philosophical endeavor but as a useful tool for translating worldview presuppositions into practical principles, rules, and guidelines for practical choices. Ethical analysis that leads to sound justifications can also be useful in communicating good reasons for choices, thereby influencing others to join in implementing them. Proficiency in ethical analysis is definitely an important requirement for good leadership.

But it is a mistake to believe leaders are primarily meditative decision makers. Leaders must be action-oriented to get followers to do what it takes to get a job accomplished. Leaders at every level focus their time and efforts on influencing others (Gefland et al. 2007). Interpersonal communication takes up from 40 percent (Simpson 2006) to approximately two-thirds of a manager's time (Stewart 1970; Mintzberg 1973). Although good leaders desire to be ethical as well as effective, they generally do not have the luxury of pondering over the theoretically optimal choice for every decision they have to make in real time with imperfect information. As one university president recently said, "Too often it is difficult, if not impossible, to apply an overriding ethical system to individual situations and circumstances" (Romesburg 2010, 10).

Nevertheless, good leaders can and do make sound ethical decisions. These are especially praiseworthy when there is strong pragmatic rationale, usually financial, for acting otherwise. A well-known example is the decision of James Burke, CEO of Johnson & Johnson, to recall all Tylenol capsules (then accounting for 30 percent of corporate revenues) after eight people in the Chicago area died after taking capsules laced with cyanide in 1982 (Jennings 2006).

Another example is that of Jack, senior vice president for corporate planning for a Fortune 500 corporation. He labored many years to find the right merger candidate to achieve the diversification he sincerely believed the company needed. But his chairman would never agree to any target company proposed to him. After retiring, the former chairman became terminally ill. Jack, upon visiting him in the hospital, was surprised by his former boss's greeting, "Hello, Jack—faithful to the end!" After some thought, Jack realized his former boss knew something he had thought was a deep secret. Years before, several other company top executives decided to force the chairman's retirement, believing (correctly, as it turned out) that he would never approve the major acquisition they thought necessary. These executives went to Jack to invite him to join their conspiracy. Although he had a personal and professional interest in making an acquisition, Jack immediately chose to refuse to join the conspirators, asking to be counted out of their group. The executives soon abandoned their efforts and nothing was ever said about it again, at least to Jack's knowledge. But, by his last greeting to Jack, the dying former chairman revealed that he had indeed learned of the conspiracy and of Jack's decision to remain loyal. Jack must have been very gratified, but his commendation was only a foretaste of the declaration each Christian leader would like to hear from his heavenly boss, "Well done, good and faithful servant."

Most ethical decisions, like Jack's, are unpublicized and few are rewarded. What motivates a person to prevail over strong pressures to compromise when the personal risks seem much greater than any compensating reward? Courageous decision makers such as Jim Burke and Jack typically cannot satisfactorily answer that. Perhaps Jim Burke really did risk his company's market share and his own position because he could see no other option consistent with the Johnson & Johnson credo—the company's first responsibility is to the people who use its products and services. His commitment to cultural integrity required the recall. As for Jack, his military experience made him respect and obey his superiors, even when doing so opposed his personal ambitions. From the perspective of spiritual and ethical leadership, their strength of will, grounded in solid moral character, ultimately disposed both of these men to act as they did. Seeing beyond their personal self-interests, they acted rationally in terms of their worldviews.

Ethical Analysis Often Is Not Difficult

No leader should avoid ethical analysis, even in cases that initially seem frustratingly complicated. In most cases, reasonable people can readily recognize a good solution or even several satisfactory ones. There are very few situations that really are hopeless dilemmas with no reachable solution. The greatest challenge often is not to decide what choice is ethically most appropriate but to actually choose and do it.

To identify a reasonable decision alternative, a person can apply heuristics or rules of thumb, such as the newspaper principle, the Golden Rule, or the Ethics Check. The newspaper principle challenges a person to ask herself if she would be comfortable seeing her behavior or decision revealed in the newspaper or other public media outlet. If not, she should reconsider before acting. For example, what if an ethics teacher were to go to a bar after class and become inebriated? If a reporter and photographer were there, he or she might publish a photo of the drunken teacher on the front page of the next day's paper. According to the newspaper principle, the teacher should consider this possible consequence before she overindulges, and avoid such behavior—if she would not like her husband, her students, and her dean to ever see such a photo report.

The Golden Rule, "And just as you want people to treat you, treat them the same way" (Luke 6:31; also Matthew 7:12) is a powerful ethical criterion. It reminds the analyst that most ethical decisions have personal implications. Indeed, C. S. Lewis (1944, 2001) shows that many religions teach this principle, which thus can be considered a universal one. The Golden Rule may not apply to all aspects of complex ethical situations, but it can help a person apply even the hardest choices with love and compassion.

In the Ethics Check (Blanchard and Peale 1988), the decision maker asks three questions in sequential order. First, is the act being considered a legal one? If so, is it balanced or most fair to all parties affected? If reasonably balanced, will the act likely offend the decision maker's conscience—can he still sleep at night? The decision maker proceeds only if he can answer all three questions positively. However, some problems occur with this approach. Being legal is not always the same as being ethical, balancing anticipated consequences can be subjective, and one's conscience is not always a good guide, for it can be hardened and seared. Puritan Richard Sibbes (1862) noted that his conscience was his best friend but also his greatest enemy.

While often helpful, none of the heuristics is adequate in every situation. Moreover, simple heuristics, such as the newspaper principle, Golden Rule, and Ethics Check, may not isolate the one optimal solution that reflects all the facts in complex social situations. Philosophers have developed various theoretical approaches to assess ethical issues and situations, and since the time of Socrates they have debated which is best. Leaders can benefit from reading the great philosophers to develop their theoretical ethics knowledge. But reasonable people do not have to be experts in philosophy to apply a basic tripartite approach that combines the perspectives of ends, means, and virtue for assessing the more complicated and difficult issues. This approach will be amplified in later sections. For most decisions organizational leaders face, they can also refer to the following straightforward model that outlines the steps in a rational decision making process.

A Model for Ethical Decision Making

Exhibit 6 outlines a rational approach for making ethical decisions. By designating fact gathering as the initial step, it differs from traditional management models that start with defining the problem (e.g., see Garvin 1993). In ethical decision making the actual problem is not always clear at the outset. This is especially the case when an individual brings a complaint about another. When an employee brings his concerns, a wise supervisor first investigates by consulting the other party(ies) and possibly other sources of relevant information to understand better what the problem really is. Then he can proceed with the rest of the process by generating alternative solutions, assessing and comparing the most reasonable alternatives, and selecting the best one or the best combination. He must think carefully about how he will communicate and implement the decision. As in all leadership models, the final phase is monitoring results and following up as needed.

Ethical leadership should be a dynamic learning process. Therefore, as opposed to an exclusive focus on the individual one-off decision, the model also highlights the importance of ethical improvement over time. In particular, it features forgiveness and an orientation toward correcting organizational structures and processes that might lead to future recurrences of ethical problems. When applied in light of a biblical worldview, as discussed in the next chapter, it offers the leader a checklist for promoting ethical transformation.

EXHIBIT 6
A RATIONAL MODEL FOR ETHICAL DECISION MAKING

1. **Get the facts.**

2. **Define the problem or ethical issues.**

3. **Generate alternative solutions.**

4. **Evaluate the alternatives.**

   o **Identify all affected stakeholders.**

   o **Anticipate consequences for each stakeholder group.**

   o **Apply ethical decision criteria:**

      • **consequential utilitarianism—costs and benefits**

      • **rights and justice—duties, obligations, moral principles**

      • **character or virtue ethics—what sort of person do I want to be?**

4. **Choose the preferred solution.**

5. **Implement the solution.**

6. **Follow up.**

   o **Evaluate results.**

   o **Correct.**

   o **Forgive.**

   o **Grow.**

Using the Decision Model

Experienced decision makers might object and say they rarely follow a traditional rational decision model—that doing so is unrealistic. They often must make tough choices quickly in dynamic, complex environments. Finding all relevant information and completely analyzing all reasonable alternatives is difficult and perhaps ill-advised, given normal limitations on time and research resources. Theoretically, a rational model assumes perfect information, the ability to identify and rank all solution alternatives using objective criteria, and the existence of an optimal solution that will provide maximum benefits to the organization and all parties concerned. This can be too much to expect in a real-world situation. March and Simon (1993) have famously said that people often satisfice using a bounded rationality model in typical day-to-day decision making. This means people tend to choose the most satisfactory alternative that will address the problem in a theoretically imperfect, but workable, fashion (March and Simon 1993; March 1994). They then apply reason to choose the most acceptable decision after a limited search for alternatives while recognizing that they do not have perfect information on the problem or on possible alternatives. The most acceptable alternative might be the one that is easiest to identify and achieve or the one that is the least controversial or safest instead of the one that is theoretically optimal.

At times, other approaches might lead to attractive solution alternatives. Sometimes the solution that proves best for long-term results is actually serendipitous, when an attractive alternative appears unexpectedly. Some people rely upon a political model, deferring to the distribution of power within the organization—perhaps for their own self-interests. The political model is particularly apt for a postmodern worldview, although it is problematic for Christians.

But the rational ethical decision-making model of exhibit 6 is recommended as a reasonable decision-making guide for supportable ethical choices, highlighting some major steps for the leader to consider. The model definitely highlights the analytical components and ethical criteria that deserve consideration. Of course it is only an outline that the decision maker needs to fit to the particular issue and environmental situation. Regardless of how a leader identifies possible solutions, if he assesses realistic ones according to sound ethical reasoning, he is more likely to make decisions that he can better justify to others. He should then be more prepared to explain the decision to others and to lead them in effective implementation. Even the most sophisticated decision makers can refer to the rational model when addressing their tough choices in practical situations.

Creative thinking or moral imagination (Werhane 1999) is still required. For the best results, experienced decision makers, like good cooks, might learn to adapt the components or ingredients or experiment to discover how (and in what sequence) they can be most effectively combined and presented. The steps of the linear theoretical model are not always completed in numerical order. An administrator needing to address an apparent problem often cannot wait for all the facts or even know all the information needed at the outset. Even when analyzing a written case, a decision maker often needs to read and reread the case to filter out the irrelevant details from the most pertinent ones for generating and choosing alternative solutions. Gathering data and other information thus should occur throughout the process, sometimes resulting in a revision of alternatives or even a redefinition of the issues and problem. Data gathering indeed should undergird all steps in the process. This often requires observation and research to weigh all the facts and opinions in light of the current context and history of the organization's personalities and relationships, cultural values and mission, economics, technology, and other areas affecting the problem. As he applies ethical criteria, the leader needs to consider the interests and responsibilities of all stakeholders, any mitigating circumstances, and his ability to act. Prayer is important throughout, and at times the decision maker should consult with wise counsel if he can do so without compromising confidences.

Even more important than making the one best, most ethically defensible decision is the attempt to make changes in policies, procedures, structural relationships, or even personnel assignments to mitigate the likelihood of future recurrences of the problem. The leader must realistically expect some imperfect outcomes based on the outworking of the Fall, but he can still attain a measure of successful ethical leadership if he and the organization learn to improve the ethical culture and the frequency of ethical shortcomings. This is why the manner of implementation and subsequent follow-up are critical. Effective follow-up requires evaluating results, implementing corrective measures, and often forgiving others. Sincere effort in this can lead to ethical growth in the parties involved, starting with the leaders and decision makers.

A Brief Comparison of Ethics Theories

If the leader is to apply the model of exhibit 6 most beneficially, she needs to have a practical understanding of the major ethics theories that are briefly described below. This does not mean a leader needs a mastery of philosophical ethics, only that she have a working understanding of the ethical principles that she can use to assess different decision choices. After getting the facts that apply to an ethical problem situation, she needs to compare possible alternative solutions to reach an appropriate decision. The basic types of ethics principles for choosing between specific acts or behaviors are consequentialism, rights, and justice. Each is briefly described below.

Utility is probably the most commonly applied consequentialist principle for decision making. One chooses the action or behavior that is expected to produce the greatest good (utility) for the greatest number. The ultimate criterion is based on measuring expected results or outcomes (the quantitative benefits less the costs) for all the stakeholders affected by an action.

Another principle, that of rights, is not primarily concerned with maximizing quantitative outcomes but serves to protect the rights and freedom of people impacted by an act. A right can be positive, such as the right to meaningful employment or education, or negative, such as the rights not to be murdered, robbed of property, or sexually harassed. People differ as to what they believe rights are, especially regarding positive rights. People also do not always recognize the responsibilities that accompany rights. If one has a right not to be sexually harassed on the job, then not only must employees not harass others, the organization's leadership has a responsibility to maintain a workplace structure and culture that minimizes the opportunity for harassment and that effectively disciplines those who harass others.

The principle of justice also focuses on responsibilities or obligations. It, like rights, is thus called deontological (referring to duties). Justice is a thick concept, having many levels of meaning and interpretations. Most basically, justice relates to how equitably the benefits and the burdens or costs of an action are shared between people or among the members of a group, organization, or society. Some see justice requiring equality of outcomes. Others, especially social conservatives and classical liberals, give greater importance to the need for equality of opportunity, a level playing field, although this will allow some to achieve more and perhaps receive greater benefits than others.

Whereas utilitarianism focuses on ends, consequences, or results, the principles of rights and justice put greater priority on duties and obligations— means over ends. Each of the perspectives considers both ends and means; they differ as to their primary emphasis. Each is also similar in being impersonal in that they do not address the personal character of the actor or the nature of the people affected. Philosophers since Socrates have debated these and their relative importance. One can become a better informed ethical leader by reading, discussing, and developing a greater understanding of how to apply these principles.

But what if in a particular situation the approaches point to conflicting decisions and acts? For example, utilitarians in some situations calculate a positive value for misrepresenting the truth—spinning or lying. In a dictatorship, should one lie to the police who are seeking to find a political opponent (e.g., a Jew in Nazi Germany) who is hiding in the house? Should the person tell the police the Jew is not there in order to protect him from unjust persecution or even a death camp? Before answering yes, he should remember that lying is morally wrong. By lying, the resident also endangers himself and the family for whom he is responsible. Answering yes in this case ultimately requires personal courage.

Most ethical decisions are not so difficult or dramatic. But a person needs to apply the virtue of practical judgment, including a large dose of common sense, to decide what decision is most ethical when considerations of consequences, rights, and justice seem to conflict, pointing to different answers.

A decision justified by utilitarian logic also can be unjust. Producing the greatest utility for a majority can cause a minority to suffer injustice. After hearing about the principles of utility and justice in an ethics class held on the reservation in Cherokee, North Carolina, one young Cherokee woman commented, "Oh, you mean it was like what happened to us?"

In the 1830s, the US government forcibly removed to Oklahoma the Cherokee and other nations who had treaties with the United States. Many died along the Trail of Tears due to cruel treatment and the incompetence of those transporting them. From a purely utilitarian perspective, however, this could be rated as a beneficial outcome. The American nation and culture was thereby able to grow westward, creating the powerful country of today. The greater number certainly benefited; some might even argue that the Cherokee people today share in the resulting benefits. However, the pragmatic ends were achieved by stealing land from civilized, largely Christianized tribes that had legal treaties guaranteeing land rights, and forcing people on a long march involving starvation, disease, and great suffering. Was this just?

Which Ethical Principle Is Best?

Philosophers can differ; often they associate with the utilitarian or a deontological camp, such as Kantian justice based on the categorical imperative. For a leader, what approach is best recommended? When should a leader or other person apply utility or a combination of rights and justice to make the practical decision that is the most ethical? Each perspective can be used to find ethical choices. But sometimes neither offers a completely satisfactory answer, especially for the most difficult ethical questions.

Nevertheless, a leader often needs to decide and act. Brady (1990) suggests that a reasonable approach is to evaluate an ethical situation in terms of each principle sequentially. This involves not only weighing the consequential benefits and costs expected from a particular decision but checking to guard the rights of each major stakeholder group impacted while seeking the most just balance or fairness to all.

As in the case of lying to those searching for the persecuted Jew in Nazi Germany, actually making the best decision may require strong character in the decision maker. This raises yet another theoretical ethics perspective— virtue ethics—which focuses on the moral character of the decision maker and actor. It recognizes that the one making a decision is a person who is subjected to pressures and personal temptations and who possesses free will. Virtue ethics is more concerned about the moral qualities (virtues and vices) and overall integrity of the person facing an ethical decision than in the specific decision to act. In virtue ethics, the question, "Are you acting as the person you want to be?" is even more central than, "Did you make the right decision in terms of consequences and means?" Virtue ethics is concerned with what it means to be a person of moral integrity and how one can grow in moral character. It brings a personal dynamic to ethical analysis that is overlooked, at least theoretically, in other perspectives.

Principles and procedures are important in leadership ethics, but they do not explain why ethical leadership is so often actually considered quite independent of such matters, most obviously when we praise a leader for being "pragmatic" or "sensitive to the needs of his or her followers" (Solomon 2005, 30). Virtue ethics, while considering the actual ethical performance of those acting, adds the aspect of their character, which is not an isolated feature of the person but rather in context is a feature of her relationships and sociopolitical roles (Solomon 2005). Rather than competing with the other theories, virtue ethics can be used to complement the principles of utility, rights, and justice (Louden 1987) through its emphasis on why a person is inclined to do (not just know) what is right and just and good, even when this involves significant personal sacrifice.

Some criticize virtue or character ethics based on materialistic interpretations of experimental evidence in social psychology (Flanagan 1991; Doris 1998; Harman 1999). Influenced from their naturalistic, closed system worldview, these critics generally charge that behavior is determined by features of the situation, not by dispositions of character traits. Robert Solomon counters these critics by pointing out that the social scientists looked at the wrong character dispositions. Miguel Alzola (2012) explains that psychologists who discount virtue misunderstand the traditional conceptualization of virtue, emphasizing the behavioral aspect of virtue to the neglect of the inner disposition. Virtue ethics is too rich to be reduced merely to situational factors. Elements of character are interrelated, but they cannot be described solely in terms of each other (i.e., in terms of behavioral dispositions). Good character is a matter of human rationality, and moral character consists of higher order desires and values, beliefs, framing capacities, emotions, and enduring patterns of behavior that have any bearing on moral matters (Alzola 2012, 386). For an action to be expressive of virtue, it must be expressive of appropriate inner states (ibid.). Christians with an open-system worldview might well acknowledge the role of spiritual influences on virtue recognition and development (e.g., see 2 Peter 1).

Currently, the important influence of moral character is gaining support even among developmental psychologists. Recent research combining moral psychology and philosophy (Pritchard 1998; and Chuck Huff and others, 2008) identify skill-based virtues of professionals in similar occupational roles (specifically, engineering and computing). Although he does not prove the existence of virtue in a strictly scientific sense, Miguel Alzola summarizes his refutation of the situationist critics, and he powerfully defends the value of virtue ethics:

> Humans may act out of character, seemingly against their overall virtuous dispositions. (For example, an honest person can at times act dishonestly.) We may fail to frame the situation as a situation that calls for a certain moral response. We may hold wrong beliefs. We may have failed to develop the appropriate higher-order desires. And our character depends in many different ways on our relations to social institutions and organizations. None of this, however, denies that character traits of the sort postulated as virtues do exist. None of this impairs our capacity to become morally better persons and attain the excellences of character that virtue ethicists call virtues (2012, 396).

A Tripartite Ethic for Ethical Analysis

Joanne Ciulla (2005, 332) points out that the following analogous perspectives, her "interlocking categories," are involved in the moral assessment of leadership:

1. The ethics of leaders themselves—their intentions and personal ethics
2. The ethics of how a leader leads (or the process of leadership)— the means that a leader uses to lead (the ethics of the relationship between leaders and all those affected by his or her actions)
3. The ethics of what a leader does—the ends of leadership

These three categories encompass virtue (character), deontological (principled means to rights and justice), and teleological (consequentialist ends) theoretical approaches to ethics. Sison (2006) and Whetstone (2001, 2003, 2006) suggest that practical decision makers combine the three basic philosophical ethical perspectives (ends, means, and virtue) within a complementary tripartite ethic. When leaders do so, they will have a complete set of tools; they can assess ethical problems according to each of the three basic aspects of an ethical decision—the anticipated consequences of an act for all stakeholders, the means of acting in terms of rights and justice, and the moral character of the actor. Often the three criteria will point to the same choice, which will strengthen the case for choosing it. If the criteria disagree as to the best alternative, the decision maker will have to draw on his experienced practical wisdom (*phronesis*) to reach a solution, often combining aspects of two or more alternatives.

For example, a divisional leader in a corporation might consider whether to reallocate a significant portion of his budget to hire a consulting firm to help develop an innovative product line. This budget shift might well be opposed by competitive divisions in the organization. The leader may find that utilitarian calculations support this new product line, projecting superior returns compared to the opportunity costs of shifting focus from his current assignments or not proceeding with other alternatives. But does the new product line support the corporate mission and strategic direction? Does the new direction fit the ethical culture of the organization? Even if it seems to be a promising fit for the corporation, does developing and marketing the new product line fall within the divisional leader's legitimate domain of corporate activity or does it impinge on turf claimed by others? The leader should monitor the consultant's activities and assure that the rights of all affected parties are protected as he moves forward. He also needs to assess the justness of cutting budgets and possibly staff to fund the consultant. Further, are both the contemplated action and the means for implementing it consistent with the image of the sort of leader he honestly wishes to be? If his answers to these questions point in the same direction, his decision should be straightforward. However, if the results are mixed, then the leader must exercise his practical judgment (*phronesis*) to weigh the relative importance of the differing criteria for the decision at hand, considering risks and opportunities to his own career and for the organization.

Leaders Can Make Ethical Decisions

This chapter presents a model that can help a leader develop practical confidence in knowing what questions he needs to answer while reaching ethically thoughtful decisions. He should benefit from informed application of the process outlined in exhibit 6 and the tripartite ethical criteria it recommends. As he gains experience, he might well adapt it to his own leadership style.

An action-oriented leader may at times find it difficult to identify one clearly right choice of action. Moreover, he often must reach a decision without much time for analysis and based on a lack of complete information. However, the leader is not condemned to pragmatic relativism. Bernard Gert (2004) explains that although there is not always one morally acceptable way of acting, in every moral situation there are morally better and morally worse ways of acting. The model for ethical analysis provides a process and basic criteria for guiding the leader desiring to find superior ethical choices. Leaders should appreciate that ethics matters and that they can be optimistic about their efforts in applying creative solutions to ethical challenges.

The next chapter reinforces this belief for Christian leaders by showing that the recommended approach for ethical decision making can be applied consistently by those with a biblical Christian ethic and worldview.

Questions for Discussion:

1. If you are seeking a genuinely good purpose, is it really so important that you use only ethical means? As an example, is it okay to cheat if this will get you the grade you need to get a job in your area of calling? Can you think of an example when any means justifies an end you consider good?
2. Christians are saved by faith through the grace of God alone, and not by works, even ethical ones. Should a Christian, knowing she has assurance of God's forgiveness and her salvation, need to

be concerned with following every principle and rule of ethics? Explain your answer.

3. Describe a situation in which you, or someone you observed, showed unusual courage in making an ethical decision. Looking back, were the personal and organizational costs resulting from that decision worth the benefits?

4. Explain why the benefits of following up a decision often can be more important than making the decision itself. Offer examples.

5. It is often not difficult to decide whether an act is ethical or not. In such cases, is it really worth the trouble to apply a rational ethical decision process before acting? When and how might a disciplined rational process nevertheless prove beneficial?

6. Thoughtful, well-intentioned people can disagree as to the best ethical decision, especially in complex situations, such as deciding how best to market a product in a highly competitive environment. Give additional examples. Should the possibility or even likelihood of such disagreement imply that ethical concerns sometimes might best be disregarded? Please explain.

CHAPTER 7

CHRISTIAN ETHICS

Without God there is no virtue because there is no moral
prompting.—Ronald Reagan

If a Christian is to serve as a leader, she needs to apply a sound Christian ethic. For this, she must possess a solid grounding in ethical understanding and the sanctified will to apply it. Such a normative ethic requires logical and sound thinking, application of the right principles for finding the truth, and dedication to act accordingly. As her first priority, she should show love for God and for neighbors by using her mind as a gift from God, seeking good reasons for what she thinks and does.

This chapter provides biblical rationale for following the ethics decision model outlined in exhibit 6 of chapter 6. A leader can possess a spiritual and rational decision-making capability if she is prepared to apply and weigh the ethical criteria of consequentialism, rights, and justice consistently based on a moral character formed according to a biblical worldview. Moral character is key as the decision maker needs to have the will and the virtue of practical wisdom to promote ethical practice effectively. Often the structural and personal support of others is important as well. However, because reasonable and spiritually minded decision makers may not always agree on one decision alternative, different individuals may well perceive situations from various perspectives and interpret and weigh the criteria differently. The approach recommended in this chapter thus is not a magic elixir nor always as straightforward as a cookbook, but it can guide the Christian who seeks to grow as an ethical leader.

The Christian Tradition Promoting Virtue

The Bible stresses that God's people are to live ethically. Worship consisting of prayer and blessing to God is a cardinal means of orienting our lives to ever increasing moral formation (Swartley 2007, 239) as those united with Christ await the *shalom* or peace of the messianic age. The Ten Commandments provide a standard for ethical living that is continued in the New Testament emphasis on personal virtues. The apostle Paul frequently admonishes Christians to cultivate qualities of virtue that are needed for sanctified living (Colossians 3:12-17; Philippians 2:2-3; Ephesians 4:2-3, 32; Galatians 5:22-23; Romans 14:17, 15:4-5; 2 Corinthians 6:4-10).

Paul identifies qualities of virtue that closely parallel those of Jesus's Beatitudes—humility and meekness, righteousness, mercy (kindness, compassion, love, and forgiveness per Paul), purity (or goodness) of heart, peacemaking (peace, tolerance, unity, patience), suffering persecution for justice's and Jesus' sake (endurance), and blessedness (joy) (Stassen and Gushee 2003). Peace is foundational to Christian moral formation, since peace is correlated with the commands to love God and neighbor (Swartley 2007, 238).

The early church fathers elaborated this virtue emphasis. Origen (AD 184-254) addressed the character qualities of virtue and the human capacity for continuous moral improvement. He sought to combine the best of ancient worldviews, such as those of Plato and Aristotle, with Christianity. Ambrose (AD 339-397) viewed the Christian life as a combination of Stoic virtues and Christian transformation. Aquinas used the images of grace and nature to weave a coherent moral theology in which grace can improve on nature (McFaul 2003, 98). He was a major proponent of moral law ethics and also of character ethics, adding the three Christian virtues of 1 Corinthians 13 (faith, hope, and love) to the four cardinal virtues (practical wisdom, courage, temperance or moderation, and justice) of the ancient Greeks. Aquinas believed every person has the freedom of will to live either according to these seven virtues or according to the seven vices (sloth, lust, anger, pride, envy, greed, and gluttony). Whereas the Reformation brought many revolutionary changes, including a frontal assault on the Platonic dualism of the Roman Catholic Church as it applied to vocational calling, major Protestant Reformers, including Calvin, retained the traditional focus on virtues as taught in Scripture.

Nevertheless, "The history of ethics may be described as largely a history of failure" (Brawley 2007, vii). This disappointing assessment rings most true when ethical directives have been imposed upon the person from the outside.

However, ethical success becomes hopeful and successful when the person is himself changed from within. Ethics can have a positive effect when it contains a focus on personal spiritual formation of moral character. Indeed, for the Christian, ethical conduct can be considered the practical outworking of spiritual regeneration and sanctification of the believer through his daily decisions and behaviors.

Ethical Transformation

Christian ethics is transformational, resting on the presupposition that people who are Christians will become transformed in their thinking and acting in ways that reflect their allegiance to Christ (McFaul 2003). Through education that is Christ-centered, it involves the transforming of the minds (Romans 12:2) of believers. It thus has a higher aim than simply to facilitate adjustments to the culture of relativism with a passing attempt to create acceptable behavior (De Jong 2001). This transformation can be seen as part of the sanctification process that operates through the gracious guidance of the Holy Spirit over the lifetime of the believer.

Christian ethics is thus a spiritual form of ethics that defines the nature of the good from the perspective of the Christian faith (McFaul 2003). Such an ethic can be a complex and confusing process, a difficult transformation that sometimes leads to differing interpretations. It may even appear as foolishness to the non-Christian. It truly makes sense only to those who are born again as new creations in Christ. This is why a person needs to accept Christ's offer of salvation before he can fully learn and practice a Christian ethic. Then he can seek to embrace Christian leadership, for which Christian ethics needs to be central (Machen 1987).

Christian transformational ethics acknowledges four major frameworks of ethical reasoning: faith-love ethics, moral law ethics, justice-liberation ethics, and character ethics. Each framework recognizes that the will of God is involved, finding expression through human reason. Christian ethical ideals are anchored in an image of Christ who reveals the nature of God's will (McFaul 2003, 6). In faith-love ethics, the divine will is disclosed through faithful or loving actions. Moral law ethics sees God's will best expressed in principles, laws, and rules. The just treatment of all persons is the emphasis of justice-liberation ethics. Character ethics focuses on living virtuously as the way to imitate God's righteousness. Each of these frameworks requires acknowledgement of Jesus Christ as the exemplar who reveals the nature of God's will, either primarily through his love or through his role as the perfect law giver or as the perfecter of justice who frees the oppressed.

For McFaul (2003), transformation ethics combines the best aspects of all four frameworks into a larger conceptual perspective for arriving at moral judgments, developing a Christian moral imagination. Such an ethic is integrative in that it seeks to explain the nature and origins of Christian moral disagreements and how to go beyond them. It is not relativistic but seeks to arrive at the best moral outcome among alternatives, more than one of which can be good.

In faith-love ethics, actions are morally justifiable if they serve as expressions of faith or love (Galatians 5:6). John Wesley, Dietrich Bonheoffer, and Joseph Fletcher are identified with this ethic. Rules can matter but are not primary. Flexibility and adaptability are essential in a dynamic world. Christ is a living presence, and personal feelings of this presence guide the Christian who is seeking to walk in faith. Those regarding love as the supreme value—even greater than faith—seek to do what is most loving in any situation. Loving others is commanded by God, but is this essential approach sufficient for a practical ethic? God is love but also is just. Therefore, an ethic that stresses loving above all other concerns, such as Joseph Fletcher's (1966) situation ethics, is simply too subjective; it can even allow a person to rationalize injustice.

Arriving at a moral judgment according to moral law ethics can be approached in two ways: the prescriptive, which follows certain "dos" and "don'ts," and the procedural, which follows a set of rules rather than prescribing specific behaviors. This distinction is analogous, except for the spiritual dimension, to that between act and rule utilitarianism. Prescriptive moral law ethics presumes that God has revealed the internally consistent, coherent principles, laws, and rules for living. These include natural laws for all of creation and moral laws for human creatures. Moral laws are universal, but specific rules (such as regarding proper dress) can change based on time and situation, although they must remain consistent with the most general principles. The *Didache* (1970) and *The Rule of Benedict* (1931) exemplify this approach. Augustine and Aquinas were greatly influential proponents of moral law ethics. Calvin (1960) agreed with Luther (1931) that the moral law is a constraint against evil, but he also emphasized that the moral law serves as a guide, a tutor that points sinners to the need for Christ (Galatians 3:24) and spiritual sanctification.

Rather than starting from a fixed framework based on the moral law as the prescriptive approach does, the procedural approach tends to follow a checklist of considerations before making a moral judgment. Challenges to the procedural approach arise due to novel situations and changing cultures (e.g., global pluralism and political economies) and technology (e.g., cloning and telecommunications advances). Such dynamic realities undermine any static approach.

Justice-liberation ethics is often heavily influenced by a Marxist-like orientation that is opposed to inequality of wealth and power. Various formulations tend to presuppose the need to oppose abusive relationships of conflict between groups in society. Marsilius (1280-1343) and Thomas Muntzer, leader of the failed German peasants' revolt in 1525, and the Levellers and Diggers in England in the sixteenth century were early radical spin-offs of the Reformation that brought together ideas of justice, liberation, and equality of property ownership by members of society. Rauschenbusch's (1912) social gospel influenced James Cone's *Black Power and Black Theology* (1969) which, using the justice-liberation framework, demands an elimination of all forms of injustice against African Americans. Christian feminist Rosemary Ruether (1972) calls for liberation with an inclusive vision based on the reconciliation of the oppressor and the oppressed (McFaul 2003, 136). Such forms of justice-liberation ethics focus on changing social structures and environment rather than on the values of faith and love, moral laws, or personal virtues and vices. Whereas Scripture stresses the problem of the righteousness versus unrighteousness of individual humans (Psalm 1), while also condemning injustice (Amos 5:16, 24) and the misuse of riches (James 5:1-6), justice-liberation ethics identifies the major moral problem instead as lying outside the individual, in the unfairness or unjustness of societal structures and human mental constructs. The justice-liberation perspective thus focuses on major ethical problems but lacks the open-system orientation of a comprehensive spiritual ethic.

The concept of the virtuous or righteous self is central to character ethics. Its focus is not on rules or changing contexts or even primarily on specific acts. Instead, the Christian should develop a moral character (or moral compass) with the right inner dispositions or virtues to guide and incline him or her to act appropriately regardless of circumstances. The morally virtuous person will be habitually disposed to know and act in the right way, at the right time, for the right end. Virtues must be learned and practiced over one's lifetime, in the manner of Aristotle's teleological ethic. For the Christian, sanctification is a spiritual process in which character is developed through efforts to imitate Christ and His virtues (note 2 Peter 1:4-9), a process that never ends or reaches perfection in this life.

Some influential philosophers, such as Friedrich Nietzsche, argue against the possibility of embracing transcendent ideals, "the idols of metaphysics" such as virtue, truth, and beauty (Ferry 2011). Recently, others have criticized virtue ethics based on interpretations of experimental evidence in social psychology (Flanagan 1991; Doris 1998; Harman 1999), basically charging that human behavior is determined by features of the situation, not by dispositions of character traits. Robert Solomon (2003) counters this by pointing out that the social scientists looked at the wrong dispositions. Alzula (2012), through a devastating critique of the misdirected attacks of social scientists, provides a strong defense of the possibility attaining the excellencies of character that virtue ethicists call virtues. Most generally, deniers of the reality of virtues succumb to the fallacy of ignorance, being blinded from nonmaterial reality by their naturalistic worldview presuppositions. Indeed, those subscribing to a closed worldview likewise reject the existence of a transcendent God because God's existence cannot be proved materially or philosophically.

But any ethic requires at least the perception—though not necessarily material reality—of standards of right and wrong, good and bad, virtue and vice. Secularists look to cognitive standards such as utility or rationally defensible moral principles. But theists look to standards from a source outside the material universe, one that those holding an open-system worldview might acknowledge is the transcendent and immanent God. A Christian thus cannot subscribe to a closed worldview limited to material consequences and rational human ideas. A Christian ethic must derive from an open worldview that acknowledges the spiritual dimension, one that impacts on humans dwelling in creation. The Christian also believes that the unique sovereign God can choose to reveal or direct humans to perceive and seek understanding of virtue and truth.

Because a Christian worldview necessarily leads to an ethic recognizing a spiritual dimension, a Christian's ethic is irrational if he does not acknowledge the ethical role of God the Holy Spirit. Objective values such as virtues, truth, and beauty can exist—although imperfect, fallen humans may define them differently and may never be able to define them with perfect accuracy or as God established them. Moreover, as Price (2006) observes, virtue ethics is problematic if it implies that leaders can infer they have less need for the constraints of generally applicable moral requirements than do their subordinates. Christians can and do fall short in this regard, even though they are exhorted to humility rather than hubris.

In summary, critics can find any human concept of ethics, as well as its practical application, susceptible to weakness. McFaul sees the strength of the faith-love ethic as its recognition of the dynamic nature of social interactions. Flexibility and moral imagination are thus needed. However, any exclusive focus on faith and love tends toward relativism in moral judgments and behaviors unless grounded in an objective foundation of principles, rules, and laws. Otherwise it can lead to contradictory rather than consistently virtuous behavior due to a greater dependence on emotional reaction than reasoned consideration. The strength of the moral law ethic is its emphasis on laws, principles, and rules. However, it can be inflexible, applying fixed rules to changing situations. Character ethics focuses on development of the inner person as a moral agent, one with the virtues that dispose the person to act in morally desirable ways. McFaul criticizes proponents of the latter view as too optimistic concerning human nature and insufficiently attentive to the need to emphasize moral law, recognize social changes, and rectify social injustices. A more apt criticism would be that virtues are culturally contextual in their definition and their development.

For McFaul (2003), transformation ethics combines the best aspects of all four frameworks into a larger conceptual perspective for arriving at moral judgments, developing a Christian moral imagination. Such an ethic is integrative in that it seeks to explain the nature and origins of Christian moral disagreements and how to go beyond them. It is not relativistic but seeks to arrive at the best moral outcome among alternatives, more than one of which can be good.

Alternatively, because each theoretical perspective has weaknesses as well as strengths, perhaps the better course for a person is to forgo philosophical formulations and simply to imitate God (Ephesians 5:1). Christians are not commanded to adopt a particular philosophical formulation, but instead are exhorted to walk without any immorality or impurity or greed, without filthiness and silly talk or course jesting or covetousness or idolatry (Ephesians 5:3-4). Indeed, Jesus Christ personally demonstrated how a person can live without sinning, establishing the perfect ideal for a Christian's ethic.

The Virtuous Example of Jesus Christ

Some Christians have studied leadership by looking to the example of Jesus Christ as recorded in Scripture (e.g., Jones 1995; Manz 1998; Briner 1997; Ford 1991; Marshall 2003; Sanders 1994). Much can be learned from such approaches, and this has long been a fruitful endeavor, as demonstrated by Thomas à Kempis's *Of the Imitation of Christ* (1965) and Brother Lawrence's *The Practice of the Presence of Christ* (1982).

However, Jesus had a unique status and calling, and the correlation between today's work and His is less than some writers suggest (Banks and Ledbetter 2004, 81). Laura Beth Jones, Charles Manz, and Bob Briner, for example, fall into the trap of approaching Jesus through the lens of modern Western assumptions, especially by individualizing the content and application of Jesus' approach, and tend to apply his teachings and practices without sufficient reference to contemporary work structures and processes (Banks and Ledbetter 2004). Lord Cadbury warns that,

"Not even the use of Jesus' own terms prevents an almost complete modernizing of him. In fact, to use them in a modern sense only deceives ourselves and others into thinking that we are accurately representing him" (Cadbury 1962, 9). Comparing Jesus to the twenty-first-century salesperson is perhaps a false simile.

Instead of attempting to clone Jesus' methods in the contemporary business environment, a person needs to seek to develop her character according to the virtues of Christ (2 Peter 1:4-9). She then can strive to fulfill her ethical responsibilities in her contemporary context as disposed by her spiritually-directed, though admittedly far from perfect, character. A Christian can be optimistic that her faithful efforts will bear fruit, knowing that God is sovereign and is beneficially in control (Romans 8:28; Matthew 6:31-34).

Nevertheless, each Christian must also know himself and others. Whereas all humans are created in the image of God and are worthy of mutual respect, none is righteous (Romans 3:10). No human creature on earth can expect to imitate the perfect example of Jesus. Christians are forgiven by the undeserved grace of God (Romans 8:1), not due to their own strivings. The unique power of a practicable Christian ethic is that, being forgiven, one can and must forgive others (Mark 11:25-26; 2 Corinthians 2:10). A person of genuine Christian character, having the mind of Christ and proper humility, should strive to do no less.

Character Development—Essential but Not Sufficient

It is thus proposed that each Christian seek to develop the virtues needed to carry out his calling. Calvin (1960) taught that responsible stewards should practice frugality, moderation, sobriety, honesty, humility, and abstinence while avoiding the vices, including excess, vanity, ostentation, greed, dishonesty, avarice, and pride. Christians do this, not as works but to thank, praise, and glorify God for His grace.

However, focusing on virtue ethics or character ethics is not always readily accepted; it was largely abandoned by Enlightenment and Modern era philosophers and scientists. Nevertheless, character ethics recently has seen a revival, promoted by philosophers such as Elizabeth Anscombe (1958), Philippa Foot (1978), Alasdair MacIntyre (1985), and Robert C. Solomon (1994), and theologians such as Roman Catholic Robert Johann

(1968) and Protestants Stanley Hauerwas (1974) and James Gustafson (1971). Hauerwas, in particular, sees the Church, Scripture, and the development of Christian character as interwoven. These authors adopt open-system worldviews and focus more on the process of character formation than on lists of specific character qualities or principles.

One way to overcome distortions due to the creep of contemporary assumptions and paradigms is to read and meditate on godly wisdom such as that found in Proverbs (Whetstone 2008a). The reader can absorb and apply the teachings of Proverbs to his present situation and problems, perhaps in ways reflecting his own incomplete understanding and distortions, but at least without the filtering often hidden in secondary sources. The great value of periodic reading and rereading of the wisdom literature is not in developing formulas for today's policies and applications but in the process of enhancing one's virtuous judgment for making reasoned and spiritually based decisions.

But whereas a character perspective is vital, it is still insufficient for a comprehensive Christian ethic. Indeed, Price's objection that virtue ethics is often misapplied may be seen as further justifying the need for formulating a more comprehensive Christian ethic. Since neither a focus on love or on justice is sufficient either, perhaps a superior transformational approach is one that reflects all three important ethics perspectives in a complementary fashion. The following section argues that a comprehensive Christian ethic should not simply be a traditional virtue ethic but be understood as a tripartite spiritual ethic that also incorporates both a teleological purpose for organizing virtues (e.g., faith/love) and deontological principles or rules (e.g., moral law) serving as complementary constraints on the means of behavior.

A Tripartite Ethic for Spiritual Leadership

As discussed in chapter 6, Sison (2006), Whetstone (2001, 2006), and others recommend that leaders apply a tripartite ethic, one that combines the character virtue, rights and justice, and consequentialist perspectives to assess ethical situations sequentially. These three perspectives comprehend Ciulla's (2005) "interlocking categories" that are involved in the moral assessment of leadership. She explains these as the intentions and personal ethics of the leaders (analogous to virtue ethics), the process or means that a leader uses to lead (analogous to rights and justice), and the purposeful ends of leadership (analogous to teleological consequentialism).

Scripture supports a tripartite formulation for Christian ethics. God, through Moses, reiterated the people's obligation to obey the moral law (deontological), which requires a righteous heart within them (character virtue), in order to achieve God's intended purpose for them (teleological consequentialism). Micah 6:8 refers to justice as God's purpose, kindness as the means (rule for right behavior), and humility as the nature or character orientation of the actor. Jesus used the image of the heart, and Paul wrote several lists of virtues forming the nature of the righteous heart. Faith from spiritual regeneration is the essential starting point for the process of sanctification developing the inner heart to obey the moral law (Philippians 2:12-13). The proper attitude for practicing the fruits of the Spirit (Galatians 5:22-23) is humbleness (not boastful, challenging one another, envying one another) (Galatians 5:26).

Morality is more than right or good acts. Scripture places greater importance on moral virtue and character than it does on rules of conduct (Holmes 1984, 116). The righteous man (1 Samuel 16:7; Psalm 119) and the pure in heart (Matthew 5:8) alone are acceptable to God. After a person is reborn—justified by the faith given by God's grace and united with Christ— then he can begin to develop some qualities of the divine nature. He can work diligently to develop the virtues or moral excellences of knowledge, self-control, perseverance, godliness, brotherly kindness, and love. If these qualities are increasing, they render one useful and fruitful in the true knowledge of our Lord, Jesus Christ (2 Peter 1:8). Having the advantage of experiencing God's forgiveness, Christians should employ forgiveness in ethical decision making. Moreover, a Christian ethic needs an independent principle of justice to insure equitable distribution of good, in addition to the principle of love or benevolence that maximizes good consequences.

A comprehensive Christian ethic thus is to include the three theoretical perspectives of teleology (faith-love), deontology (moral law), and virtue (character). No one perspective is evidently dominant for all situations, but all are required and supported for practical application of a biblical Christian worldview. And combining the strengths of multiple frameworks is nothing new, having been demonstrated by many, from

Moses to Reuther (McFaul 2003). The Christian leader should consider all three theoretical viewpoints, deciding how to act most ethically by applying practical judgment (Whetstone 2001, 2006).

Applying the Ethical Approach

The Christian leader can adopt the tripartite ethical decision-making process as a rational approach consistent with Christian theology. Application includes the logical process steps of defining the problem, generating alternative solutions, selecting one or a combination of the alternatives, and developing a plan for implementation. The decision maker assesses the alternative decision choices by applying each of the three ethical criteria in turn: (1) the anticipated results or consequences of an act (outcomes); (2) the means used in acting (rights, justice based on moral law); or (3) the disposition arising from the moral character of the person acting (virtue).

When the respective criteria differ in choice of the best alternative, the leader must call upon his experience and prayer-informed judgment to decide on the most appropriate criterion, and thus the alternative that it favors, for the situation at hand. The differing ethical perspectives also help inform the decision maker as to the way he administers the choice he ultimately makes. For example, when justice for the group and community require sacrifice or even reprimand of one of their number, love and mercy may be needed to ease or at least partially compensate the pain endured for the greater good. The leader might reprimand privately an employee who takes excessive lunch breaks, allowing him an additional opportunity to conform to the time set apart for lunch. This shows respect and concern for the employee. If he does not improve thereafter, the leader might decide to administer additional punishment to provide justice to other employees, who have already had to bear the extra burden of his initial lateness.

Another example is the dilemma of the Christian university dean who wishes to offer a faculty contract to a Christian PhD in a discipline for which doctoral positions are hard to fill, such as accounting or healthcare administration. Because he is unable to offer a fully competitive salary due to institutional pay scales, the dean considers agreeing to a reduced course and faculty service role for the candidate. If the position is in accounting, this will allow the person hired to supplement his income by continuing to maintain a separate accounting practice while teaching several critical courses. The dean considers the benefits of providing the students excellent teaching, thus meeting accreditation standards, to outweigh any negatives. Moreover, he expects that accounting course enrollment and future recruiting of majors will bring significant quantitative benefits to the university.

In making his decision, the dean might have to consider other factors as well. Assuming institutional policies allow for the arrangement as described above, are the reduced load and service requirements fair to other full-time faculty members? Will others see the dean's exceptions in this case as being impartial or unjust? Are the action contemplated and the means for implementing it consistent with the sort of leader the dean wants to be—a Christian who manifests biblical moral character? If his answers to these questions point in the same direction, his decision should be straightforward. However, if the results are mixed, then the leader is called upon to exercise his practical wisdom (phronesis) to weigh the relative importance of the differing criteria for the decision at hand. As a spiritually minded leader, the dean should bathe the entire decision process in prayer.

A leader with a Christian worldview should also realize that sound rational analysis, while vital, is not the greatest challenge for the leader who seeks to be ethical. Doing what one knows is right is often existentially more difficult than knowing what the right action is. Sound application of theory is essential, but ethical behavior in a fallen world requires much more. Human capacity to rationalize, as well as the complexity of many situations, can cloud the issue and frustrate the leader needing to make a decision. Indeed, most people's motivations are a complex mix of self-interest, altruism, and other influences. Derry (1991) observes that an act can still be ethical even if it involves mixed motives, if it is good for the organization's interests while also serving the leader's self-interests. Nevertheless, a leader is spiritually wise to consider the advice of Joseph Butler in his "Self-deceit":

> There is not any thing, relating to men and characters,
> more surprising and unaccountable, than this partiality
> to themselves, which is observable in many; as there

is nothing of more melancholy reflection, respecting
morality, virtue, and religion. Hence it is that many men
seem perfect strangers to their own characters. They
think and reason, and judge quite differently upon any
matter relating to themselves, from what they do in cases
of others where they are not interested. (Butler, 1726,
398-99)

Humans tend to avoid serious self-examination. For example,
recognizing a potential conflict of interest that involves oneself is more
difficult than recognizing conflicts of interest involving others. As in all
decisions, the Christian's most important source of guidance is rational,
prayerful meditation on Scripture. Every Christian leader should also
be willing to subject himself to the audit and control of others, such
as a board or other counselors. The appropriate attitude of the ethical
Christian is that of humility, recognizing his need for repentance and
gracious forgiveness (1 Peter 5:5-7) and expecting spiritual help as a
response. Christians also can profit from what Alexis de Tocqueville
(1969) wrote on Kant's condemnation of a person using the language
of ethics as a screen or tool for self-love and self-interest (Aeschliman
2007). A person can slip into this *radical evil* (Kant's term) almost without
noticing. To avoid this temptation, Christians should guard against
flippantly using "church language" and attributing their willful desires
to the leading of the Holy Spirit (i.e., telling others "God told me to do
this"). The Holy Spirit does guide men (and women), but God wants us
to test carefully whether a desire, even one that seems to further what
a person may firmly believe is a good overall purpose, is really justified
ethically and biblically (see Acts 17:11). Making a disciplined effort to
prepare a sound ethical justification also can help a leader better explain
the reasons for a decision to others, including non-Christians.

In summary, an ethically and spiritually minded leader should both
apply self discipline to learn ethical decision making concepts and strive
to develop strength of moral character for applying them. Effectively
using a comprehensive tripartite ethic requires the leader not only
to apply logically the right principles for finding the truth but also to
dedicate her will to act accordingly. Christian ethics is a demanding and
continuing challenge. But if a person possesses the attributes discussed

in this part III, including the fifth attribute involving the technical leadership competencies of an effective and ethical leader (highlighted in chapter 2), the reader can be optimistic that she (or he) can succeed as a transformational ethical leader. Doing so should not become a source of pride but instead reflect the proper humility of the leader who recognizes the grace of God as her source of strength.

The next chapter further describes the overall role and responsibilities of a Christian leader. Meeting these will challenge the technical effectiveness, ethical sensibility, and spiritual mindedness of the person called to lead well.

Questions for Discussion:

1. For the Christian, ethical conduct can be considered the practical outworking of spiritual regeneration and sanctification of the believer through his daily decisions and behaviors. Thus, God gives us the rational ability to act ethically.

   But do you believe that a non-Christian also can be ethical? Do you know any ethical non-Christians?

   If you say yes, does this suggest that God's (Father, Son, and Holy Spirit) spiritual help is not needed for one to be ethical? **or** Does it mean that God as spirit sometimes chooses to develop (even within some non-believers who are unaware of God's spiritual influence) moral character qualities and the willpower needed for seeking ethical behavior?

2. This chapter poses that moral character development occurs through a spiritual transformation within the person. What, if any, examples of this have you observed?

3. Are personal humility and forgiveness highly valued in the culture of your workplace? Even if they are not, how can you remain humble and demonstrate a spirit of forgiveness as you seek a successful career?

4. This chapter also proposes that a comprehensive Christian ethic should combine the strengths of a faith-love ethic, God's Moral Law, and Christian virtues. What are the strengths, and the limitations, of each of these approaches?

5. The "tripartite" ethic is suggested as a comprehensive approach wherein the decision maker tests alternative choices against each of three criteria: (1) anticipated outcomes or results, (2) rights and justice, and (3) virtue. Often the criteria agree as to the best alternative. However, if the best answer differs depending on the criteria used, the decision maker can draw upon her experience, wisdom, and common sense, seasoned with prayer, to weigh the alternatives. After referring again to the case example at the end of this chapter, think of another ethical problem you have personally confronted. Would the "tripartite" approach have been helpful to you in analyzing this problem? Explain.

CHAPTER 8

THE CHRISTIAN
AS AN ETHICAL LEADER

All the ways of a man are clean in his own sight, but the LORD
weighs the motives. Commit your works to the LORD, and your
plans will be established.—Proverbs 16:2-3

A Demanding Challenge

*B*uilding on the previous discussions of ethical, effective, and spiritually minded leadership, this chapter describes the role and responsibilities of the Christian leader. It suggests biblical answers to some of the multitude of challenges to expect.

When a Christian is called as a leader, at first he may resist, but God has a profound, sometimes mysterious, way of using instrumental means to accomplish His will. He endows the leader with natural proclivities and providentially prepares him through education, training, and experiences. The called leader also is encouraged through circumstances and appeals from followers and others. The Christian who assumes any leadership role, however, is rarely as well qualified as he can be. He should thus commit to enhancing his knowledge, relational skills, and moral character. A biblical worldview should guide his ethical behavior as he supports others in resolving problems, making and implementing decisions, and molding followers' characters. As he strives for effectiveness in his role, he should ever seek to lead from the perspective and toward the furtherance of a Christian spirituality—for the honor of his ultimate Master.

An old saying is that leadership is lonely. But this is not actually the case for the Christian, because his Lord is ever with him (Matthew 28:20). He thus should dedicate himself optimistically to his responsibilities with persistent endurance, even in times of defeats and discouragement. If he truly loves others, he can draw on inner motivation even when he feels unloved.

However, if the leader eventually senses a change in his calling, such that his leadership responsibility should be transferred to another person, he should be ready to move on, having done all he can to have equipped others to replace him. Once he leaves his leader role, he should become a loyal follower or withdraw completely, not allowing himself to become a stumbling block or competitor for the new leader.

Being a successful spiritual leader is a challenging aim. Christians do not always succeed in engaging their faith in the workplace. Perhaps this is because the contemporary church often does not adequately prepare them through instruction or by example. Pastors often neglect to teach their members how to apply biblical principles in the workplace, possibly because seminaries do not equip them to do so. Moreover, Nash and McLennan in *Church on Sunday, Work on Monday* (2001) observe a gap in understanding between the Christian ideals of pastors and the realities experienced by the working people in their congregations. Perhaps pastors should learn from experienced business people, and focus more on encouraging their congregants to draw upon and share their own practical insights for workplace applications of worldview principles.

A Spiritual Endeavor

A person with leadership responsibilities does not become a spiritually minded leader by tacking spiritually onto his leadership approach. The person's spirituality is foundational; he or she must first of all be spiritually faithful and obedient in order to integrate spirituality with leadership behavior.

A Christian, leader or not, can believe that her spiritual-mindedness gives purpose and meaning to life and all of life's spheres, including the workplace. Christian conversion requires knowing oneself as a sinner needing grace for the salvation that comes only from God. Subsequent growth in sanctification, though often with apparent lapses as well as recoveries, involves a lifelong deepening of self-understanding. The believer learns that her primary purpose, in the words of the Westminster Standards, is to glorify God and enjoy Him forever. Her proper attitude is to rejoice always, pray continually, and in everything give thanks (1 Thessalonians 5:16-18). Her ethic is to seek to do justice, love kindness, and walk humbly with her God (Micah 6:8). As a steward, the Christian has an awesome responsibility over God's creation, which she is to order and enjoy (Genesis 1:28).

Every believer's sacred responsibility is to obey God's commandments, chief of which is to love God with all her heart, soul, mind, and strength (Mark 12:29-30). She also is to love her neighbors as she loves herself (Mark 12:31), with "neighbors" understood to include those of other religious persuasions and even enemies. Therefore, she is interconnected with all men and women, who are also created in God's image—and thus are to be treated with dignity and respect. This indeed is a sound starting point for any ethic as well as an explanation of social meaning. It precludes a natural selfish form of self-interest, instead leading to a moral concern for community, social justice, and environmental stewardship.

Growth as a spiritual Christian is a learning process through spiritual application of truths revealed in nature and in God's special revelation in Scripture. Each Christian grows in worldview understanding, although this takes time and study and can involve varying interpretations due to human limitations and sinful inclinations that remain even in those of faith in Christ. Even when he seems to experience difficulty, discouragement, and a lack of inner peace, the Christian can know that the God of peace is with him and that Christ will bring perfect shalom to all the earth when He returns in glory. While waiting for this glorious event, believers can remain assured that the Christian experience leads to peace with God, a peace that is beyond human understanding.

In a Christian worldview, spirituality and ethics are interwoven. Christian faith and biblical ethics are thus incompatible with a closed system worldview. The sovereign God is in providential control over all His creation and its history. He is transcendent—unlimited by the natural—and He also immanently intervenes in man's domain and indeed, in the human's most inner being, thoughts, and actions. For the Christian, realistic, objective study of nature through science is essential, but a believer also can respond to the spiritual influences upon him, depending on God's biblical standards for guidance and on God's personal help for ethical application. For this, a person needs spiritual balance; a Christian should neither be a legalist or an antinomian. A popular spiritually sound ethical test for the Christian is to ask himself, "What would Jesus do?" and then do so (1 John 2:6).

No Christian, whether leader or follower, can honestly claim that he meets all the above requirements. Jesus Christ alone lived a perfect life. All other humans sin (Romans 3:23), and all of creation is fallen (Genesis 3), which are two well demonstrated empirical facts. Because Christians still sin, they must continually confess and repent so God will cleanse them from unrighteousness (1 John 1:8-10). But the Christian can trust in God's sure promise that there is no eternal condemnation for those who are united by faith in Christ Jesus, for the law of the Spirit of life has set him free from the law of sin and death (Romans 8:1-2).

The leader nevertheless needs to be watchful and discerning. It is the height of folly for Christian leaders or followers to act under the assumption that others, believers or non-believers, will always speak the truth and conduct their business as Christ would. Even those with the best of intentions are limited in knowledge, perception, ability, and sensitivity to others. Even faith-based organizations do not always act as Jesus would act in their business relations, with employees or external constituencies. Christians sometimes expect too much of other believers and naively drop their guard, suffering as a consequence. C. S. Lewis's *The Screwtape Letters* (1942) is thus profitable reading for Christians seeking to be good leaders.

The Christian as Leader

A Christian should seek to glorify God in whatever he does (1 Corinthians 10:31). If called as a leader, the Christian should seek excellence in his exercise of leadership. He is to practice a rational and spiritual ethic, grounded in a biblical worldview, which should guide him in his behavior. He should avoid sexual immorality and refrain from profane language, and seek to act according to a reasoned, biblical worldview for the purpose of glorifying God, lovingly demonstrating respect for his fellow men and women (Mark 12:30-31).

The spiritual leader influences others not by the power of his own personality alone but by that personality irradiated, interpenetrated, and empowered by the Holy Spirit (Sanders 1994). Leadership is enhanced by natural endowments and traits of personality, such as intellectual capacity, force of will, and enthusiasm. But according to Oswald Sanders (1994, 20), the real qualities of leadership are to be found in those who are willing to suffer for the sake of objectives great enough to demand their wholehearted obedience.

The leader's aim should be to excel in leadership behaviors in his organizational or social role and in the application of a biblical ethic. In this, he will err in boasting or presuming success. His more appropriate attitude is that of humility; he may honestly feel that he never becomes more than a work in progress. Most definitely, the Christian should not use his profession of faith or his Christian manner of life to excuse him from excelling in the high standards for being an effective leader as outlined in chapter 7. He should also accept the specific leadership challenges highlighted below.

Biblical Leadership Lessons

Scripture abounds with lessons and examples of good leadership. A good leader should use power appropriately (especially power over himself) (Proverbs 16:32). He is to exercise control and discipline properly (Philemon 8). He must acknowledge his accountability to proper authority and others (Luke 20:25) and motivate others without manipulating them (Psalm 40:1-8; 2 Corinthians 5:14-15). He is to communicate carefully—honestly and clearly—while listening to others (1 Timothy 4:11-16).

Chewning et al. (1990) list the following responsibilities for a Christian leader:

- They are models of moral behavior. A tougher standard is often applied to Christians in business than is applied to others (p. 137). The believer thus needs to appeal to God for a clean heart and a steadfast spirit. (See Psalm 51:10-13.)

- They articulate and carry out the vision for the organization (p. 138). (See Proverbs 29:18.)
- They maintain open communication—clear, simple, unambiguous, and to the point (p. 139). (See Matthew 5:37.)
- They are responsible for team building, based on a high level of trust (p. 139). (See Acts 20:28; Ephesians 4:11-12; Matthew 28:18-20; Luke 10:17-20.)
- They create environments that encourage and facilitate growth and creativity (p. 140). (See Matthew 28:18-20; Luke 10:17-20; Philippians 4:6-13.)
- They also manage the functions and procedures of an organization (p. 140). (See Exodus 18:17-27.)

To succeed, leaders need to develop their inner strength and character. They also seek fruitful development of their followers, including skill development and improvement in decision-making ability, as well as increased collaboration, a feeling of support and challenge, and greater productivity and character. Good leadership depends on good followers who respond creatively to leadership and are productive, creative members of the team (Crockett 1976). Honesty and trust are to be priorities among leaders and followers.

Practical applications abound, and the leader can learn from a variety of sources. He needs to weigh all relevant information, different viewpoints, and competing interests in making sound judgments. This involves the Greek virtue of *phronesis*, or practical judgment, which is developed from experience, and by integrating Scripture into decisions. For example, a veteran army sergeant taught this author never to bow to the use of profane language. He rightly pointed out that one's troops, though often profane, look with disrespect on the officer who employs such degrading language. Why indeed should followers respect a leader who shows a lack of honor for his family and his God? It is wise to seek out and listen attentively to trusted counselors (Proverbs 13:10, 19:20), such as the wise sergeant.

Certain character qualities are normative for Christian leaders, indeed all spiritual leaders. Chewning et al. (1990, 133-37) use the Beatitudes of Matthew 5:3-9 as a checklist of the inner personality characteristics of Christians. This list, however, does not exhaust the virtuous characteristics of Christian leadership. For example, the fruits of the spirit (Galatians 5:22-24) also give practical directions for leaders who are to exercise their virtues with the attitude of humility (Galatians 5:26).

God speaks forcefully against the shepherds of Israel who use their positions to further their own interests rather than feeding or caring for the needs of the flock (Ezekiel 34). Paul warns masters—whether in the home or the marketplace—not to exploit their power over followers but to treat them with justice and fairness, since they too are subject to the impartial God (Ephesians 6:9; Colossians 4:1).

Instead, a good leader needs to assume the responsibility for establishing structures and culture that will promote ethical behavior and lessen temptations and pressures to unethical practices. This requires good communication using means appropriate for the context. For example, he should seek to deter sexual or other forms of harassment and must discipline offenders. He should strive to see that strategic and budgetary objectives do not pressure employees to engage in unethical practices. He should establish incentive systems rewarding group and organizational achievement rather than destructive interpersonal competition. The properly humble leader does not manipulate his followers or abuse his position. Rather, he refrains from overworking and exploiting others for his personal career success. He is wise if he seeks to bless his followers and strangers in need (Isaiah 58:7), serving as an exemplar of concern for others.

And the leader must always remember that all eyes are upon him. He cannot expect to hide long from exposure through the grapevine, and he never escapes the complete knowledge of his Lord. He and other leaders must comply with organizational and professional codes of ethics, policies, and procedures. If any code of ethics is to be effective, it requires the support of the consensual cultural values of the organization's members and consistent application of code requirements throughout the organization, from top to bottom. If the leaders are not monitored as closely as employees on the firing line, or if they are given exemptions not understandable to others, then even the best code or policy quickly becomes merely window dressing. Even the most well-intended structures and culture cannot endure hypocrisy, which Rochambeau described as "the tribute vice pays to virtue." The leader should pray that he will provide his followers no justification for charging him with dishonesty or hypocrisy.

Regular prayer fortifies the spiritual leader and empowers his leadership. The teacher prays for his students; the businessperson prays for his employees, superiors, customers, and competitors, and a minister prays for the members of his congregation. The late Dr. John Reed Miller, a Presbyterian minister, exemplified the prayerful leader. His youngest daughter, Priscilla, recalls that each Sunday morning he would spread his sermon notes on his bed and pray at length for the Lord's blessing and empowerment. He would shed tears for his people's salvation and their daily life challenges as he lay, arms outstretched, over the words he would deliver. This intelligent, strong, and gifted leader was humbly following the example of King Hezekiah, who prayed over the letter from Sennacherib demanding Jerusalem's surrender (2 Kings 19; Isaiah 37). Both Dr. Miller and King Hezekiah rank as Level 5 (highest) leaders in terms of Jim Collins's (2001) twin requirements of proper humility and consuming ambition for the success of their organizations.

Leadership Influence by Those in Junior Positions

How can a Christian not in a CEO position be an effective spiritual and ethical leader? Does any person have any realistic hope of changing the culture when he is in a middle management or junior position? A bright young Christian student once raised this practical concern, asking "How can I, as a junior employee, help influence and change my secular workplace where my supervisor and the other employees are not Christians?" The reality is that a person will not be able to perfect or even quickly reform his organizational culture if it is not already inclined toward spirituality. Nor should he struggle to do so to the point of frustration. Nevertheless, he can demonstrate a sanctified character through his consistent behavior, obeying his boss and serving his organization (Ephesians 6:5-9; 1 Peter 2:18ff) without transgressing the moral law or his calling as a Christian (Acts 5:29). He must remember that God placed his superiors as governors over him (Romans 13), although he ultimately serves the Lord (Colossians 3:23-25).

A Christian at any organizational level, even the junior employee, can be optimistic, however, that he can eventually make a positive difference through his consistent and persistent example. The Jewish tenet of *tikkun olam* reflects considerable practical wisdom: a person should not strive to perfect the whole world but merely work to leave the place and the people he meets a little better than he found them. Proper humility involves a realistic commitment to achieve moral progress while assigning credit to God—but without "wearing Christianity on your sleeve." Unbelievers seem to identify and watch the Christian more than one realizes. Indeed, Christians sometimes notice that others hold them accountable to higher professional standards and personal behaviors than those to which they seem to hold themselves and others.

But due to sin and human limitations, everyone sometimes falls short. A Christian ethic requires repentance and requests for forgiveness— from God, coworkers, and others. Demonstrated repentance and requests for forgiveness are ultimately empowering rather than signs of weakness.

A Good Leader Must Also Be Effective Technically

A Christian called to a leadership position should never presume to be a good leader just because he is committed to applying a sound Christian ethic based upon his worldview. He must also be proficient in applying leadership techniques, styles, and models. The knowledge and skills he needs come from common grace insights and experience. A Christian should not assume he does not have to work and study to learn how to improve and grow as a capable leader, one who can earn the respect of his followers and others in the world. He should strive to be an effective and ethical leader, as discussed in chapter 2.

Meeting the Leadership Challenge

Whether junior or senior in his organization, a Christian is to be winsome and set an example of excellence that honors Christ. As the Christian matures and gains respect from employers and coworkers, he may well gain influence in technical and ethical matters. He may earn promotion to more responsible organizational positions. In the meantime, he can remember relational and other workplace experiences and their lessons so that he can draw upon them to create a more ethical, God-honoring culture when given greater executive or administrative authority.

Every spiritually minded leader should humbly seek out the ethical ways to positively influence the world in his sphere of responsibility. He needs to develop the knowledge, technical skills, habitual practices, and moral character required. Proper humility is not weak or fearful but is consistent with a positive, honest assessment of one's capacities to contribute—without pride or boastfulness.

The appendix offers essays that discuss how biblically grounded approaches can help leaders successfully address workplace issues they are likely to face. These issues include

- how to communicate a vision;
- the essential importance of being honest and trustworthy;
- how to delegate;
- why loyalty still matters; and
- whether it is time to quit and move on.

These issues often involve difficult choices requiring thoughtful and prayerful consideration by anyone facing such existential decision situations. However, the Holy Spirit will strengthen and reassure the faithful leader facing these and many other practical challenges. Success comes from constantly remembering that it is Christ whom you serve (Colossians 3:23-24).

Questions for Discussion:

1. Do you believe that you are called to be a leader—at home, at work, at church, in the community, and/or on the national and international stage? What evidence do you have to support your belief?
2. What is required to be a good follower? Are you a good follower? Offer examples from your experience.
3. How do you rate yourself as a leader? When considering your answer, refer to scriptural examples of leaders and the responsibilities of a leader (note Chewning et al.'s list as quoted in this chapter).

4. What character qualities or virtues do you believe you need to develop further to be a spiritually-minded, ethical, and effective leader?

5. How do you try to avoid the vice of pride, which is a great failing of many otherwise successful leaders? What does humility in an effective leader look like?

PART IV

GROWING AS A
GOOD LEADER

*T*he reader now may be saying, "I agree with much of the previous theoretical discussion describing what it can mean to be an effective, ethical, and spiritually minded leader, but how can this help me personally?" Or another may be saying, "I already practice much of what this book preaches, but I would like to improve in certain ways." The next two chapters offer some practical suggestions for such readers.

Chapter 9 asks the reader to consider what leadership style to adopt. It focuses on an analysis of servant leadership, which is often promoted as the best approach for Christians. However, it does not recommend servant leadership for everyone. Each leader needs to decide on the style he should adopt, based on his individual assessment as to whether servant leadership or another leadership style best fits his personality, role, and situation.

Chapter 10 presents specific practices a person can use to develop and grow as a better leader. The reader can adopt some or all of these in his individual leadership and character-development plan.

CHAPTER 9

ASSESSING SERVANT LEADERSHIP

It is not so among you, but whoever wishes to become great
among you shall be your servant, and whoever wishes to be first
among you shall be your slave; just as the Son of Man did not
come to be served, but to serve, and to give His life a ransom for
many.—Matthew 20:26-28

Some, especially Evangelical Christians, proclaim servant leadership as the preferred style for leadership. Christ exemplified servant leadership in his ministry (Isaiah 53; Matthew 20:26-28) and urged his disciples to first serve one another (John 13), and Christians are exhorted to imitate Christ. However, Scripture does not declare any particular leadership style or technique as normative for every person. What style should a spiritually minded leader adopt for his individual role, responsibilities, and situation? This chapter examines servant leadership, critically assessing its inherent strengths and weaknesses. This analysis can help the aspiring ethical and spiritual leader to decide how and when he might adopt servant leadership or possibly look to other leadership approaches.

Servant leadership is commended by a wide variety of proven leaders. Margaret Thatcher's advisor Lord Brian Griffiths (2005, 36) says, "Arguably, the highest form of leadership is servant leadership." He explains that leadership cannot be separated from the needs and concerns of the followers. The same theme emerges strongly in Sam Walton's autobiography. This iconic discount retailer stresses no less than three times that servant leadership was the ideal he sought in running his business (Walton and Huey 1992). Even in the horrors of battle, a leader can be a servant. Major Dick Winters, who is immortalized as the leader of *Band of Brothers* (Easy Company, 506th Regiment, 101st Airborne Division, US Army) (Ambrose 1992) demonstrated the heart of a servant. His view of leadership was finding "that peace within yourself, that peace and quiet and confidence that you can pass on to others, so that they know that you are honest and you are fair and will help them, no matter what, when the chips are down" (Anderson 2004). Servant leadership is an admirable style, one worth investigating further.

What Leaders Seek through Servant Leadership

As a normative theory, servant leadership seeks to develop moral character and meaning. As explained in chapter 2, servant leadership leads to a culture of spiritual growth, whereas transformational leadership leads to an empowered dynamic culture (Smith, Montagno, and Kuzmenko 2004).

The Bible depicts Jesus Christ as a sacrificial, loving servant leader (Matthew 20:28). Many Christians look to servant leadership as the optimal paradigm for ethical leadership and spirituality, but servant leadership is not inherently theological. Its practice is not exclusive to Christianity or any specific religion or worldview.

Indeed, Robert K. Greenleaf's (1977) servant leadership is a nonsectarian philosophy that supports people who first choose to serve, and then to lead as a way of expanding service to individuals and institutions. Servant leaders may or may not hold formal leadership positions. The difference between the leader who is leader first and the one who is servant first is the latter's care to ensure that other people's highest priority needs are being served. "The best measure of its success, though one difficult to administer, is: Do those served grow as persons? Do they, *while being served*, become healthier, wiser, freer, more autonomous, more likely themselves to become servants? *And*, what is the effect on the least privileged in society? Will they benefit or at least not be further deprived?" (The Robert K. Greenleaf Center for Servant Leadership 2011).

Greenleaf acknowledges the influence of Hermann Hesse's (1956) *Journey to the East*, an account of a mythical journey in which a servant named Leo performs menial chores for the group of travelers and sustains them with his positive spirit and song. All goes well until Leo suddenly vanishes. The group then falls apart and the journey is abandoned. The narrator of the story years later encounters Leo, who from the outset actually had been the great and noble leader of the order that had sponsored the journey. In developing his normative concept of *the servant as leader*, Greenleaf draws on the moral of this story: that the greatest leader is one seen as a servant first, and that fact is the key to his greatness.

The essential element of servant leadership is not temperament, strength, or energy but the leader's source of motivation. She is motivated by the potential benefits to the followers and the needs of the organization, rather than motives revealing pride, manipulation, and force (Nelson 1996). Nelson depicts the relationship of the servant leader with others as a horizontal one among peers. Greenleaf (1977) prefers a *primus cum pares* ("first among equals") relationship.

The methods preferred for a servant as leader are persuasion and personal example. There is no preferred style or unique formula, however. A servant leader can have any of the sixteen Myers-Briggs personality type preferences (Lewis, Spears, and Lafferty 2010). The leader needs to abandon his preconceptions of how best to serve and listen as others express their needs. A leader builds people through service when he genuinely puts other people first, viewing them as humans worthy of dignity and respect. The process of change starts within the leader. When a problem arises, the servant first looks within himself for the cause and then works to develop solutions without ideological bias or preconception. Leader success is measured by the positive growth in others, the people served and, most especially, the least privileged in society.

The practice of servant leadership therefore is a matter of the outworking of character rather than leader technique or style. Since it concerns relationships, good results require receptive response from followers, peers, and superiors. Introducing servant leadership to a culture will not assure improvement, however, unless the culture is prepared to be receptive (Matthew 9:17; Mark 2:22).

An Assessment of Servant Leadership

Servant leadership offers important benefits to a leader-follower relationship. However, critics identify disadvantages as well. A discerning leader is wise to acknowledge both the strengths and the weaknesses as he decides on a personal style. The following discussion can help inform a person considering whether or not servant leadership best suits his personality and leadership situation.

Benefits

The benefits of servant leadership are those generally associated with normative leadership theories that seek to refocus leadership thinking on the importance of virtuous character of leaders, a perspective overlooked in traditional social science research (Yukl 2010). These theories include servant leadership, transformational leadership (Burns 1978), spiritual leadership (Chappell 1993; Fry 2003; Kriger and Seng 2005), and authentic leadership (Avolio and Gardner 2005; George 2003). Interest in these theories has increased recently, possibly in reaction to corporate scandals and declining confidence in elected officials (Yukl 2010, 420). Servant leadership places high value on encouraging a relationship of trust and cooperation. According to the Greenleaf Center, a leader builds trust, loyalty, and satisfaction by demonstrating the following personal characteristics: listening, empathy, healing, awareness, persuasion, conceptualization, foresight, stewardship, commitment to growth of people, and building community (DeGraff, Tilley, and Neal 2001). Subordinates respond with more organizational commitment, willingness to carry out requests, and enhanced perceptions of distributive and procedural justice when their leaders have these characteristics. As an employee-oriented servant culture develops, it allows followers to adopt servant leadership themselves, encouraging them to develop the character of a servant. This culture of trust then tends to attract talented and committed employees.

The particular advantages of servant leadership are its altruism, simplicity, and self-awareness (Johnson 2001). It emphasizes a moral sense of concern for others, reducing the complexity engendered by putting personal desires in conflict with those of followers. A servant leader applies moral imagination (Werhane 1999) as he listens to others and engages in an ongoing conversation from which emerges a shared vision, and a better one (Kiechel 1995, 125). Nevertheless, before a person selects any style to adopt for leadership, he should consider its weaknesses as well as its potential strengths.

Criticisms

Craig Johnson (2001) observes that the servant leadership approach (1) seems unrealistic; (2) encourages follower passivity; (3) doesn't work in all contexts; (4) can serve the wrong cause; and (5) has a negative connotation to slavery. Perhaps even more unsettling is Norman Bowie's (2000) objection that servant leaders are susceptible to being manipulated by followers. These and several other possible disadvantages are addressed below.

First, is servant leadership unrealistically optimistic? Genuine servant leaders are rare, but extraordinary people have nevertheless met the challenge. Greenleaf (1977) offers the example of John Woolman, who in late-eighteenth-century America adopted the vision of abolishing slave ownership. He spent thirty years traveling up and down the American East Coast, discussing the morality of slavery as he visited fellow Quakers. His efforts succeeded as the Society of Friends voted to forbid the practice of slavery, becoming the first religious denomination in the United States to do so.

Another servant leader was Nikolai Frederik Severin Grundtvig, the Father of the Danish Folk High Schools. For fifty years in the nineteenth century, he passionately advocated these schools as a means whereby Danish peasants could prepare themselves to be full participants in their nation's culture, freely voting and owning land. What he gave was his love for the peasants, his clear vision of what they must do for themselves, his long articulate dedication—some of it through very barren years—and his passionately communicated faith in the worth of these people and their strength to raise themselves—*if only their spirit could be aroused* (Greenleaf 1977, 34). Aung San Suu Kyi, the Burmese scholar and wife of an Oxford professor, is a contemporary exemplar of servant leadership. Overwhelmingly elected president of Burma in 1990, she was not allowed to serve; the country's military rulers arrested her and for years restricted her freedom. She used the $1.3 million awarded her with the 1991 Nobel Peace Prize to establish a health and education trust for the Burmese people. Declining to renounce politics, she has continued to seek to persuade the world of her country's cause for freedom, recently realizing some success.

Each of these leaders sacrificed over much of their lifetimes for a worthy but practical vision. The standard they set is extremely high for the average mortal person. But Woolman, Gruntdvig, Suu Kyi, and others have demonstrated that genuine servant leadership is within human possibility for those with the will to persevere in it.

Second, Johnson suggests that human nature may incline some followers to rely too much on a sacrificial leader. However, if practiced successfully, the servant leader paradigm establishes a culture that encourages followers also to become servant leaders, not merely to remain as passive subordinates. The leader uses persuasion and sacrificial example to inspire others to join with him in conceptualizing and implementing a consensual vision. He does all within his power to grease the skids for others, but he still must promote responsible relationships. He cannot merely provide a valet service, waiting upon every whim and perceived need of his team, but has to challenge others to take responsibility for difficult tasks. If critics are correct in attributing follower passivity to servant leadership, this indicates that some would-be servant leaders stress fellowship and service at the expense of the overall welfare of their teams and their mission. A genuine servant leader instead must demonstrate the integrity of character needed to overcome follower passivity.

The third of Johnson's criticisms is definitely on target. Leadership research (Bass 1990) finds that the most effective leadership style varies with the situational context. Some roles and situations, such as that of a prison guard or a military commander in combat, may appropriately call for more autocratic behaviors and greater top-down discipline than is associated with a servant style. Moses proved wise when, following the advice of Jethro, he established a hierarchy of able men to help him judge the Hebrew people in the wilderness (Exodus 19:17-27). He was able to delegate authority and responsibility effectively by limiting his access, allowing others to share his burdens. Moses' labor was easier and his people were served better—a win-win situation. Although this great leader was truly humble (Numbers 12:3), having the nature of a servant, he did not restrict his approach or style to that typically associated with servant leadership (also see Numbers 16:3). Servant leadership therefore is not optimal at all times in all circumstances. A leader needs to adapt to his assigned role and the situation without compromising his ethical commitments. This is the case even if he tends to follow servant leadership for most routine situations.

Johnson's fourth objection applies to every kind of leadership. Any approach is flawed if the leader seeks the wrong purpose or cause. Normative paradigms that direct the vision and commitment of followers toward misplaced aims are dangerous. Servant leadership and transformational leadership are especially so because they are motivationally effective. Moses was unable to enter the Promised Land as leader not because of his flawed organization, as Greenleaf (1977) claims, but because God disciplined him for his momentary lapse into the sin of prideful disobedience when he struck the rock twice (Numbers 20:12). He had lost sight of his own true role and purpose as the leader of God's people. A genuine servant leader understands that he is called by a higher authority to serve others and he strives to follow his call consistently. If instead of falling into hubris, the servant leader listens, cultivates trust, and humbly promotes a consensual vision through persuasion and example, there is reduced likelihood that he will stray toward a lesser vision. As Rabbi Wayne Dosick says, "If we uplift the human spirit, we can bring meaning and value to the modern marketplace" (Iwata 1995, 128).

Fifth, is the term *servant leadership* itself a hindrance? Shirley Roels (1999) explains that *servanthood* sometimes connotes self-effacement and other-determined ways of operating, ones having more to do with servitude than with service. *Shepherd leadership* is an alternative, one that connotes the attentive care and compassion of a shepherd. Indeed, Christ refers to Himself as the *Good Shepherd*, never as a good servant leader.

Peter Block (1987) prefers the use of stewardship language versus servant language. He contends that people should see their role as primarily a trustee of something valuable, one who is to pass it on to the next generation with added value. According to Banks and Ledbetter (2004 109), Block says,

Stewardship involves moving from patriarchy to partnership and from security to adventure. To achieve this leaders must move beyond dominance and wish for dependency and be willing to make full disclosure and develop more inclusive managerial practices, develop capability among employees, and build widespread financial accountability throughout the organization. This results in the creation of a balance rather than a hierarchy of power within an organization, a commitment to the entire community rather than to individuals or teams, empowerment of all to help define the organization's purpose and ethos, and an equitable rather than an unbalanced distribution of rewards.

Achieving Block's depiction requires a spiritually directed emphasis on service through stewardship. If *servant leadership* connotes something else, then there would be merit in renaming it. However, the designation *servant leader* is well established in the literature. Leaders and academic proponents may find it difficult to rename it but still can stress that genuine servant leadership should not imply support for slavery or servitude by social inferiors.

Perhaps the most troubling objection is that servant leaders are too susceptible to manipulation by followers (e.g., Bowie 2000). A genuine servant leader, however, does not bend or fall to such manipulation. Instead, he is concerned, even to the point of personal sacrifice, that his fellows are empowered, equipped, and motivationally united in pursuit of the mutually agreed upon mission. And if such a culture is not yet achieved when hard choices need to be made, the servant leader must be willing to stand up for objective truth and what he perceives is right. While favoring persuasion over harsher and more impersonal methods, he nevertheless should be unwilling to submit to manipulation or obfuscation in the interest of team spirit and collegiality. If he does, he may well continue to call himself a servant leader, but is he not quite different from Block's steward leader or a faithful shepherd?

The case of Umaru Musa Yar'Adua illustrates some practical difficulties of genuine servant leadership, including the problem of manipulation. This man promised to be a servant leader when he took his oath as president of Nigeria on May 29, 2007. According to *The Economist* (July 21, 2007), this approach to leadership was his announced, and apparently sincere, hope for solving Nigeria's most pressing problems: insurgency and gangsterism in the Niger Delta oil fields, erratic electric supplies, and massive corruption. But the beleaguered president was under conflicting pressures to serve the interests of both Nigeria's powerful political factions and the allies of his predecessor. The new president lacked the trust of many Nigerians because his election had been patently rigged. Yar'Adua furthermore suffered from a kidney ailment. He resorted to prevarication and delay in appointing his ministerial team from among the candidates, who included backers expecting to be paid off and people foisted on him by his predecessor. Meanwhile, the problems of lawlessness, falling electricity output, and demands for looting the state's finances intensified. In reality, how likely was it that he could prevail as a servant leader?

Genuine servant leadership will likely require the leader to take stands that her superiors or followers do not appreciate at the time—if ever. When the leader does not bow to the special interests or myopic agenda of her followers, she can lose their esteem and trust. Indeed, she can lose her followers. An extraordinarily articulate communicator (such as Ronald Reagan) can take difficult positions and retain collegiality from friends and reasonable foes, but this is extremely difficult for most leaders with career ambitions. The challenge increases when opposition arises due to hidden and self-centered follower motives that the servant leader cannot or is unwilling to confront with gentle persuasion. At the very least, she must possess an extraordinary strength of character to persevere when faced with lack of recognition from superiors and loss of affection from followers. Perhaps this is why so few men or women are widely acknowledged as genuine servant leaders.

Organizational Cultural and Structural Challenges

Effective practice of servant leadership is dependent on the environment in which the person leads, including the culture and structure of his organization. Ideally, a servant leadership culture permeates all levels of the organization, promoting and facilitating the exercise of servanthood. Banks and Ledbetter (2004) point to companies such as Herman Miller,

ServiceMaster, and TD Industries as positive exemplars worthy of further study.

Managers at any organizational level can adopt a servant leader approach. This requires their taking responsibility for what they delegate, depending on others for wisdom, being willing to take a stand in the interest of others and the organization even at the cost of their positions, and being willing to sacrifice for others as well as their organization. Unfortunately, many of the greatest and most costly sacrifices may not be recognized. But the true servant leader is willing to take this chance, for that is what servant leadership requires.

Servant leadership can be especially difficult for the middle manager or subordinate leader. Even when servant leadership is a professed cultural value of the organization, administrative management tends to emphasize numerical profitability goals and compliance with bureaucratic policies. While essential, competitive market objectives and regulatory compliance concerns can diminish the recognition and reward for servant leadership approaches perhaps desired by the manager and expected by subordinates. If the department manager claims to be a servant leader, but submits to top-down pressure to increase workloads and reduce resource costs, his subordinates may conclude that he is a hypocrite, more intent on pleasing his superiors than representing their interests. Such a middle manager is thus squeezed by the structure of the organization. Can he maneuver between the "Scylla" of risking the trust of his superiors as a loyal administrator and the "Charybdis" of risking the trust of his department?

Furthermore, top leaders in churches and religious organizations, as well as those in businesses, tend to act pragmatically rather than as committed servants, merely co-opting the language of servant leadership for their own agendas and purposes (Banks and Ledbetter 2004). Those in organizational authority tend to place the main emphasis on being leader rather than on being servant. Nevertheless, the fact that something is often abused or misused does not mean it has no value as a normative standard or even as a realistic possibility within an organization. But the requirements are challenging.

Essential Requirements for Becoming a Servant Leader

If a person claims to be a servant leader, he must recognize and seek to overcome the problems associated with this approach. He must promote a consensual vision and require that his followers fulfill their relationships responsibly. His mindset and the techniques he adopts must fit the situational context suitable for servant leadership, and the leader must be able to assure that he is not susceptible to manipulation. If the overall culture and structure of the organization support the leader in these endeavors, his task remains difficult but is at least more realistic. If not, then the leader should consider adopting another approach.

A major distinction between servant leadership and other views of leadership is that for a person to become a genuine servant leader, his very nature must be changed. Servant leadership is not merely a style of leadership but more essentially refers to the nature of the leader (Marshall 2003). The leader's will-to-power should focus on power for others, not power for self or power over others (Marshall 2003). Greenfield (1977) also says that some spiritual driving force must be behind the motivation to serve. Servant leadership thus is best recognized as a spiritual approach.

As he serves with proper humility, the Christian can help his followers grow in character and as servant leaders as they work together to fulfill a mission. Over time he can learn and reap practical benefits. For example, his Bible study might convince him to pay his employees promptly (Leviticus 19:13) and adequately (Luke 10:7), thus building subordinate loyalty.

The first priority of the servant leader, however, is not other people (subordinates, other fellow workers, or superiors). He strives for harmonious relationships, but his objective should not be harmony at all costs. He must stand up for principled truth, perhaps being misunderstood rather than praised and sometimes being subjected to undermining opposition. Indeed, a genuine servant leader should not naively expect to be universally understood or honored.

Nor is his highest priority, although an important one, the successful accomplishment of his organizational mission (Acts 5:29). The greatest priority of the biblical leader is serving the Lord Jesus Christ (Colossians 3:23-24), which requires drawing on a spiritually endowed strength of character (Philippians 4:13).

Since the requirements are very challenging, it is not surprising that there seem to be few genuine servant leaders. Moreover, the typical organizational culture does not support a consistent exercise of servant leadership. Therefore, despite its promised benefits, servant leadership is too idealistic to be recommended as the primary style for all leaders in every situation or even as the approach expected for the leaders in a particular organization. Nevertheless, servant leadership can serve as a guiding standard for spiritually minded leaders who have the required strength of character, the nature of a servant.

Should Every Christian Be a Servant Leader?

Christians might find it quite reasonable that they should be servant leaders. Nelson (1996) says, "Servant leadership is at the heart of Christian leadership." Some Christian colleges even proclaim in their mission statements a commitment to equip servant leaders. A Christian leader should not only seek to live according to a biblical worldview and follow a sound Christian ethic as she grows in spiritual sanctification, but she should strive for technical competence in applying leadership knowledge and skills.

However, not every faithful believer called to a leadership role can be accurately described as a servant leader. For example, the leadership style of Moses differed from Greenleaf's concept of servant leadership. He excelled because "the man Moses was very humble, more than any man who was on the face of the earth" (Numbers 12:3). Justification by faith does not give one all the skills and developed character needed for servant leadership. Another approach might reasonably be more appropriate for some leaders.

Moreover, even though England's Lord Griffiths' (2005) view that "A true leader is a servant leader" may be good advice, it is best understood only in a general sense. Indeed, Griffiths identifies typical servant leader behaviors that echo those recommended by Kouzes and Posner (2004) for exemplary Christian leadership: model the way, inspire a shared vision, challenge the process, enable others to act, and encourage the heart. These behaviors are not exclusive to servant leaders; they certainly fit secular formulations of transformational leadership, as well.

In considering what leadership approach to adopt, a Christian should also note that contemporary formulations of servant leadership are not all biblically derived, nor are they empirically demonstrated. Greenleaf was significantly influenced by Hesse's (1956) fictional account of a spiritual and geographic journey led by Leo, the prototype of a servant leader. But this is not a Christian account; the servant leadership program of the Greenleaf Institute is humanist rather than explicitly Christian. Moreover, Yukl (2010) observes that there still is little empirical evidence in support of servant leadership, that most evidence as to the effects of servant leadership is anecdotal and based on case studies of historical leaders (e.g., Graham 1991). Thus, the case that a Christian leader should always apply a servant leadership approach cannot be supported unequivocally. Servant leadership is not always the best approach. An ethical and spiritual leader might also beneficially adopt other approaches, such as transformational, charismatic, or even non-participatory styles in certain situations and contexts.

In practice, each Christian who leads needs to recognize his own organizational role, the realities of the situation, and the organizational context when deciding how to behave and lead biblically. Because pressures and temptations are ever present in the world, where complex interactions of often competing responsibilities can make consistent worldview practice very challenging, the leader needs to build upon basic worldview thinking by applying thoughtful biblically based ethical analysis. For this, he may beneficially apply servant leadership, but sometimes he might find that another approach will also do—or perhaps even better help him serve Christ in his calling as an ethical and spiritually minded leader.

Questions for Discussion:

1. What are the benefits of leading with a servant's heart—perhaps by adopting the approach of servant leadership? Consider the personal benefits to you and potential benefits to others and your organization.

2. Although numerous successful leaders praise servant leadership, why are relatively few people widely recognized as genuine servant leaders?

3. Offer examples showing how a person seeking to be a servant leader might be manipulated by followers or by others. How can a servant leader counteract and overcome such attempts at manipulation?

4. Explain why and how servant leadership might best be understood as a spiritual approach?

5. Do you agree that some Christians might find that servant leadership is not always the most appropriate approach for them, that another leadership style better suits their role and organizational context? Explain.

6. Do you desire to be a servant leader in your organizational leadership role? What do you see as the greatest benefits and the most difficult challenges you will experience? If you sense the calling to lead as a servant, may the Lord bless you mightily.

CHAPTER 10

DEVELOPING LEADER CHARACTER

We make men without chests [hearts] and expect of them virtue and enterprise. We laugh at honour and are shocked to find traitors in our midst.—C. S. Lewis, 1944

So far, this book has emphasized a theological and philosophical discussion of ethical leadership and spirituality, supplemented and illustrated with practical examples and techniques for the aspiring leader. This final chapter offers practical guidance for the person who asks, "How can I develop the moral strength of character I need to be an effective, ethical, and spiritual leader?"

The best answer is ultimately up to each aspiring leader, as he depends upon the providential leadership of God. There is no straightforward checklist of deeds to perform or degrees to earn. Nor is the key to success found by focusing legalistically on rules. Developing as a good leader is most of all a Spirit-led endeavor that develops personal character in terms of the qualities a person needs to fulfill his calling at work, in the home, and as a citizen. This requires him to understand the importance of moral character and to identify those qualities he needs to cultivate through spiritually guided effort.

Although he will not approach perfection in this life, the person seeking to grow in virtue can become more habitually disposed to know, act, and lead in the right way, at the right time, for the right end.

As Aristotle taught, virtues must be learned and practiced over one's lifetime. For the Christian, character development is part of a lifelong, spiritually-empowered effort of seeking to imitate Christ and His virtues (2 Peter 1:4-9).

Virtues Needed by a Spiritual Leader

Virtues are character qualities that dispose a person to act in the appropriate manner toward a good end. Which virtues does a leader need to perform in his calling with excellence? Exhibit 7 lists the four classical virtues and some biblical ones. Calvin (1960) taught that responsible stewards should practice frugality, moderation, sobriety, honesty, humility, and abstinence while avoiding the vices, including excess, vanity, ostentation, greed, dishonesty, avarice, and pride. Chewning, Eby, and Roels (1990, 133-37) use the Beatitudes in Matthew 5:3-9 as a checklist of the inner personality characteristics of Christians. Research among American food store managers and executives finds that personal honesty ranks above all other traits in the workplace (Whetstone 2001, 2006). Beabout (2012) suggests that all these empirically identified traits are connected to practical wisdom (Aristotle's *phronesis* or Aquinas's *prudentia*)—the central trait needed to pursue the excellences that are internal to management as a domain-relative practice. A person of practical wisdom has developed excellent habits of deliberation, judgment, and execution (Beabout 2012, 419). The aspiring leader should assess his personal strengths and weaknesses in reference to each of these admirable qualities. He then can focus on where he chooses to improve.

Recently, however, theologians have focused more on the overall process of character formation than on lists of specific character qualities or principles. An individual in today's complex society should not arbitrarily choose a specific universal list of idealized virtues without assessing them in light of his own role and organization. The most appropriate list, the relative importance, and even the contextual meaning of virtues needed by a leader to excel may vary according to the leader and his role in his organization's culture (Whetstone 2006). Moreover, character development can augment and empower one's practice of a duty-based ethic that constrains and guides moral decisions and character development according to the moral law and revealed scriptural principles. Most importantly, whatever set of virtues a person identifies for development, he is to commit himself to the Christian's organizing purpose, serving Christ through his work (Colossians 3:23-24).

Developing as a Leader of Moral Character

Character and specific character qualities can be taught and developed, not just at a young age but also in young adulthood and even throughout one's lifetime (Rest 1986). Whereas traditional instruction through lecturing is generally ineffective for molding character, there are more effective methods. Schools and business organizations can foster character development among willing students and employees, respectively, by establishing and maintaining a supportive structure and culture, identifying role models, praising the exercise of good character, promoting mentoring, and stressing challenging assignments without condemnation for failure (Lockwood 2009).

The process of character development is complex, too much so for comprehensive investigation here. Scholars do not always agree as to the most effective methods. Nevertheless, in the following pages the author suggests the following beneficial practices based upon research and his own experience as a teacher and manager.

- accepting challenging assignments
- engaging a personal character mentor
- reading thought-provoking literature, especially biographies
- observing other leaders in action
- keeping a journal to record and assess leadership observations and experiences

But because each aspiring leader is created as a unique individual, ultimately he must decide how best to customize his personal development program for developing the character qualities he most needs. He might find benefit from all or instead prefer to adopt some combination of these habitual practices, each of which is briefly described below.

Accepting Challenging Assignments

People reveal their true character under pressure, but they also grow when they are pressed to perform new and difficult tasks. Just as a person strengthens his muscles through habitual rigorous exercise, he can seek to develop his virtues by habitually striving to think and act virtuously—in the right way, at the right time, in the right place, to a right or good end. Through deliberate, habitual practice, a person can develop his increasing disposition to act according to the virtuous standard to which he aspires. On the other hand, just as the slothful "couch potato" can see his muscles atrophy, the moral person can grow less virtuous or even vicious by relenting to temptations to act selfishly or according to other vicious behaviors.

Charles R. Swindoll illustrates how adults can productively challenge youth with his story of the musician Ignace Jan Paderewski. Present in his concert audience one evening was a mother with her fidgety, squirming nine-year-old. The mother had brought her son in the hope that he would be encouraged to practice the piano if he could just hear the immortal Paderewski at the keyboard.

> As the mother turned to talk with friends, her son could stay seated no longer. He slipped away from her side, strangely drawn to the ebony concert grand Steinway and its leather tufted stool on the huge stage flooded with blinking lights. Without much notice from the sophisticated audience, the boy sat down at the stool, staring wide-eyed at the black and white keys. He placed his small, trembling fingers in the right location and began to play "Chopsticks."
>
> The roar of the crowd was hushed as hundreds of frowning faces pointed in his direction.
>
> Irritated and embarrassed, they began to shout:
> "Get that boy away from there!"
> "Who'd bring a kid that young in here?"
> "Where's his mother?"
> "Somebody stop him!"

Backstage, the master overheard the sounds out front and quickly realized what was happening. Hurriedly, he grabbed his coat and rushed toward the stage. Without one word of announcement he stooped over behind the boy, reached around both sides, and began to improvise a countermelody to harmonize with and enhance "Chopsticks." As the two of them played together, Paderewski kept whispering words of encouragement in the boy's ear, challenging him to play it well. (Miazza 2011)

Teachers, work supervisors, or parents can likewise challenge their charges or subordinates to succeed, directing them toward small wins and encouraging them to learn from their mistakes (Kouzes and Posner 2004).

And it is not too difficult or too late for working adults to grow toward excellence, often when they are properly challenged to leave their comfort zones. Although Hartshorne and May claimed that their research denies that virtue can be taught, their findings actually demonstrate only that instructional methods such as lecturing are ineffective for this purpose (Sprinthall and Sprinthall 1988). More recent psychological research by James Rest et al. (1986; 1988) finds that moral development continues throughout formal education, particularly among young adults. Not only can socialization neutralize and repress a person's moral character (Bellah et al. 1985), it can have positive influence as well. The formation, refinement, and modification of a person's operational value system— the attitudes and beliefs that motivate conduct—are ongoing processes throughout one's life (Josephson 1988, 28). The Christian can associate this phenomenon with the gracious, spiritual process of sanctification, which often involves tests from worldly pressures and challenges.

The leader who seeks to grow in virtue should welcome and even seek out testing assignments, including ethically challenging ones. This is not to say he should go to the extreme. He must learn to say no as well as to say yes to requests, resisting the temptation to try anything and everything to the point of exhaustion and frustration. Moreover, he should avoid assignments that he considers contrary to his worldview commitments. And if already engaged in a task that stretches him mentally, physically, ethically, and spiritually, he might have to decline or seek postponement of additional challenges until the first one is achieved. Nevertheless, he needs to accept some challenges— even risky and possibly frightening ones. His overall character and spiritual growth can benefit from his willingness to be stretched.

Engaging a Personal Character Mentor

The relational process of one-on-one or dyadic mentoring can be another means for learning how to receive and how to give wise counsel in the workplace or other social settings. It is biblically wise to seek the advice of trusted counselors (Proverbs 13:10, 19:20). The aspiring leader should deliberately cultivate a network of advisors from among her friends, family, or more experienced coworkers and superiors. She must be careful in selecting counselors and mentors, however. She needs to follow the admonition of Psalm 1 to shun the wicked who advise in ways contrary to God's Word, which is the test of counsel that will stand (Proverbs 19:21).

Based on empirical assessments, mentoring remains a well-accepted development approach for career development, material rewards, and psychological benefits. Moberg and Velasquez (2004) refer to surveys estimating that between 38 and 55 percent of employees have been mentored at least once in their careers (McShulskis 1996; Simonetti, Ariss, and Martinez 1999). Toastmasters International has long successfully incorporated mentoring, encouraging club members to share their knowledge, skills, and experience while helping new, more inexperienced members improve as public speakers.

Mentoring also can promote the development of moral character (Whetstone 2010). Indeed, mentoring by an experienced person of a more junior person has been used for character development since ancient times. Socrates and Gandhi approved of those teachers who could help people become able to learn virtue for themselves (Rouner 1993). Aristotle taught that persons of virtuous character, with relevant experience in the contextual domain of practice, can mentor others through application of practical wisdom.

Parties to a mentoring relationship can benefit one another in terms of professional knowledge and skills and in character development. Although the mentor generally offers relatively more benefits and receives relatively fewer than the person mentored, the essence of the adult mentoring relationship is *offering and receiving,* with the desired result that the mentor and mentee should each take pleasure in the enriching interpersonal exchange (Cohen 1995, ix). Moreover, a successful mentoring experience also prepares and may motivate the mentee to mentor others. Empirical research shows that mentoring participants experience outcomes that are generally positive, although both mentees and mentors have reported abuses, dysfunctions, and ethical risks (Moberg and Velasquez 2000, 2004).

Transformational leadership and servant leadership both call for the leader to nurture the character growth of followers. One recommended practice of effective transformative leaders, for example, is that after a learner makes a mistake, the leader will provide mentoring support, encouraging persistence toward improvement. Leaders who mentor also develop as they seek to be the role models regarding the standards they set for their mentees. Part of being a good leader may even be serving as an effective mentor, someone who develops others into good leaders.

Ethical concerns are central in the mentoring relationship since the process is a medium for moral advice and instruction, with mentors serving as role models for the process of moral development (Weaver et al. 2006). Both mentors and mentees have a responsibility to engage in an ethical manner, starting with a clear mutual understanding of the ground rules and objectives of their two-way offering and receiving relationship. The person mentored must take responsibility for her own growth and development, not expecting to be excused because of her junior status or the relatively greater overall responsibility assumed by her mentor.

Typically, modern educators no longer promote growth in moral virtues as a central objective for mentoring. But they are mistaken, proving guilty of the charge by C. S. Lewis (2001) that they are making men without chests (hearts) and expecting of them virtue and enterprise. Since manifesting a strong moral character is vital for ethical behavior and ethical leadership, spiritually minded leaders should seek to demonstrate strong integrity and encourage its development in others. Mentoring can and should establish a positive context for this, if mentors and mentees mutually commit to ethical behavior in their relationships.

Reading Thought-Provoking Literature, Especially Biographies

In practice, ethics involves interactive relationships among people. However, business ethics, as generally taught at the university level, focuses on identification of ethical dilemmas and decision-making skills, a cognitive and rational approach that can underemphasize the emotional, volitional, and spiritual aspects of human nature. The technical, narrow, and individualist orientation of much business ethics thus falls short of the more holistic, loving approach consistent with a Christian worldview. This at least partially explains why people frequently ask teachers, "Isn't business ethics an oxymoron?" Unfortunately, Andrew Stark's (1993) claim, that business ethics teaching is considered irrelevant by the average business practitioner, still has the ring of truth.

Some scholars have come to recognize the importance of enriching professional education by renewing its focus on nurturing the creative mind and the heart, rather than maintaining an almost exclusive devotion to technical training. Donaldson and Freeman (1994) and Walton (1994) recommend the humanizing of business education. Their view is that ethics is best—and most successfully—taught along with the value-engaging perspectives of history, philosophy, literature, languages, and intercultural studies. Solomon (1994) recommends that this include cultivation of the virtues and a concern for inspiring students to be good, humane persons. These proposals represent common grace insights similar to what C. S. Lewis wrote in *The Abolition of Man* (1944, 2001). Education should build hearts devoted to traditional, universal virtues such as courage, honor, and love of neighbor; the aim of education is to make the pupil like and dislike what he ought (Aristotle, quoted in Lewis 1944, 2001, 16).

How can a leader develop his values perspective, and thus his heart, without returning to university for a humanities degree? He can adopt the habit of reading great works of literature, including biographies and autobiographies of leaders. Reading such literature can help a person appreciate how others came to recognize and address leadership challenges. One can find edifying books, articles, and videos at the library and the bookstore; by soliciting recommendations from counselors and mentors, coworkers, friends, and teachers; and from literature reviews.

Through disciplined reading and discussion with colleagues, a person can nourish his intellect and stimulate his motivation for character development and relational skills.

But leaders are active and busy, and many are not prone to quiet meditation. Why should they spend their valuable time reading biographies and other works of literature? Time devoted to reading can be viewed as an investment, resulting in the benefits of expanded near-term knowledge and insights. Moreover, over the longer term, the reader might well grow in human understanding and wisdom. These benefits are especially important for leaders who properly seek to cultivate ethical relationships.

Observing Other Leaders in Action

An aspiring leader can also benefit from observing other leaders in action, their behaviors and also the character qualities they manifest. Furthermore, identifying the most admired leaders in an organization and their apparent character qualities might be a key to understanding and finding excellent managers in the contemporary workplace (Whetstone 2006). This suggests that, if it is carefully adapted for changing cultures and situations, a trait approach—one considered wise by many cultures over the ages (Bennett 1993; Anderson 1993)—can complement other methods in a process of character development. For example, Dietrich Bonhoeffer serves as an exemplar for investment banker Buzz McCoy. Although he discounts any over dependence on hero adulation, McCoy still confesses, "Bonhoeffer modeled all these traits [of a successful leader], leading me eventually to teach in my church, serve in a residence in a seminary, and become a lay member of a Benedictine monastery" (McCoy 2007, 15). He also identifies Harry Cunningham, the CEO who built K-Mart, as one who "exemplified the great leaders we can only hope to become" (McCoy 2007, 98). The admiration he expresses for these men causes one to wonder whether McCoy would have been able to write the thoughtful classic "The Parable of the Sadhu," or to become an effective ethics teacher, without the influences on his character development provided by Bonhoeffer, Cunningham, and others. Senator John McCain likewise extols the value of observing the exploits of exemplary leaders.

The following excerpts from his speech to US Naval Aviators at Tailhook 2011 apply universally to aspiring leaders.

> My grandfather, who commanded a carrier task force in the Pacific during WWII, lived large and was always larger than life to me… . He made it a point to talk with pilots after they returned from a strike, asking them, "Do you think we're doing the right thing?" Here was a 3-star admiral, taking time during the course of war to receive honest feedback from men under his command. My grandfather knew that if you ever stopped learning, especially from your men, then you also stopped leading…
>
> So as we celebrate the centennial of Naval Aviation and begin to contemplate the next 100 years, I encourage all of you to look back on those who led us through our first century. I urge you to study their lives and their leadership styles. Then strive to be like them. Learn to inspire the men and women who work for you. Learn to lift them up, to give them meaningful responsibility, to allow them room to grow, and yes, even to make mistakes. Be slow to judge, and remember that many of our most gifted leaders would never have survived in a "one strike" or "zero defect" environment. If instead your style is to be quick to criticize, slow to praise, and you are unwilling to forgive, I urge you to seek a different profession. And if you have not yet learned the power of redemption, I encourage you to read the biographies of Nimitz, Halsey, Boyington, Henderson, McClusky, and Waldron—just to name a few. (McCain 2011)

Trait theories of leadership postulate that it should be possible to identify those superior qualities of the leader that differentiate him from his followers. Until the 1940s, most leadership research concentrated on individual traits, but pure trait theory thereafter fell into disfavor, in part because personal traits are often poorly defined and overlapping and these approaches do not specify the appropriate intensity for applying individual traits. The personal qualities are also posed as universally applicable rather than situational and trait approaches typically do not explain how traits can be interrelated in the makeup of an individual's character. Stogdill's critique concludes that both the person and the situation must to be considered, not simply a universal set of traits (Bass 1990).

However, the tendency of scholars to write off the trait approach goes too far when they view it as exclusively a matter of universal characteristics (of every "Great Man") rather than as inputs to a process that is culturally influenced and subject to individual subjective assessment. In a study of the personalities of 316 CEOs and the performances of their companies, Kaplan, Klebanov, and Sorensen (2008) found that characteristics related to executive skills of execution and organization were generally undervalued and characteristics related to interpersonal skills such as listening and team building were overvalued. Research also has identified personal characteristics such as drive, desire to lead, motivation, honesty and integrity, self-confidence, intelligence, knowledge, and flexibility as important for leadership success (Schermerhorn 2004, 167).

Research within an American corporation (Whetstone 2003) found that experienced managers can readily identify individuals as either positive or negative role models, their most-admired or least-admired exemplars. When questioned, these managers had little difficulty describing specific cases and behaviors in which their role models— often an early supervisor— demonstrated character qualities that the responding managers valued as worthy of emulation (e.g., honesty or courage) or of suppression (e.g., dishonesty or cowardice).

An aspiring leader will naturally tend to observe others and attribute their behaviors to dispositions of their character virtues or vices. However, he needs to be careful. Character attributions can be risky—even very wrong. Attribution Theory (Weiner 1986) posits that people, including bosses, tend to attribute poor performance or failure to character vices in others, while they attribute successful performance to their own positive qualities rather than to contributions of others or favorable circumstances. An observer must discipline himself to be as objective as reasonably possible, avoiding quick judgments. He should not over generalize, but recognize that different people may not agree as to the best choice for a leadership model, and that a person may well choose different leaders depending on the situation. Nevertheless, an aspiring leader can benefit from observing others if he concentrates upon increasing his understanding and appreciation of those qualities he could enhance within his own character, while avoiding criticizing the character of others.

Therefore, whereas the universal trait (Great Man) approach is problematic, and any trait approach is at best insufficient alone, an individualized and contextualized observational approach still can be beneficial (see Deal and Kennedy 1988). Indeed, closely observing, analyzing, and emulating the moral and behavioral qualities of admirable leaders can be used to complement other methods for character development—if appropriately adapted for changing cultures and situations. Disciplined observation can be especially important for those who can find little time to read. Furthermore, close observation and interactive experiences in workplace relationships involve processes of trial, error, correction, and possible improvement that add an experience-based dynamic that reading the great books or biographies inherently lacks.

Keeping a Journal

An active person—such as a responsible leader—frequently meets memorable people and faces new problems in dynamic circumstances. When he manages to break away from his pressing responsibilities, he desires diversions and perhaps just rest. How and when can such a person focus his mind on his character development, or anything so philosophical or meditative?

Some find the answer to be keeping a journal. This simple discipline can help the leader recall, organize, and think about specific ways he can learn from his daily experiences and insights from his challenges, mentoring relationships, reading, and observations of others. Even the busiest leader should be able to allocate a short time each day for recording observations and thoughts about his leadership outcomes and ways he might improve. At the end of the day or in a morning quiet time, he can take a few minutes to record notes about the persons or incidents that made impressions on him that day. He might also jot down any leadership lessons and follow-up questions his observations suggest. Insights from prayerful reading, including Proverbs and other Scripture passages, can help him pray for opportunities for application. Over time, and perhaps to his surprise, he may well experience growth in his moral character.

The diarist can periodically (quarterly or yearly) review his journal entries. He might write an evaluative summary that highlights patterns of behavior he finds in others and in himself. Has he consistently been open to challenging assignments? Has he been able to maintain healthy mentoring relationships? Has he read as much as he hoped and has he gained helpful insights from observing others? Overall, has he enhanced the nature and consistency of his ethical responses or has he in some areas gone downhill? Over time, the journal can provide data about good, and not so good, leadership as well as a record of leadership development, perhaps stimulating the leader's growth technically and spiritually.

Succeeding as a Leader

Leading well is a great challenge, requiring the leader to dedicate his mental, physical, emotional, and spiritual resources to his vocational calling. A Christian needs to build upon basic worldview thinking by applying thoughtful, scripture-based ethical analysis and sound leadership practices as he addresses leadership decisions. Succeeding at this may appear daunting because pressures and temptations are ever present for a leader facing complex interactions of competing responsibilities. Indeed, success in leadership requires not only spiritual knowledge and insight but also integrity of character. This chapter suggests five ways of promoting development of the character a person needs to become a good leader: (1) accepting challenging assignments; (2) engaging a personal character mentor; (3) observing other leaders in action; (4) reading biographies and accounts of leadership; and (5) keeping a journal to record and assess leadership observations and experiences. Adopting some or all of these practices can help a person grow as a good leader, one who is effective and ethical.

If the leader is, by God's grace, spiritually minded, he will have an open-system perspective. According to a Christian worldview, he can recognize and respond to the influences of spiritual forces and the transcendent standards of a supreme supernatural presence as he leads at the personal, institutional, and societal levels. For a Christian, serving as an effective and ethical spiritually-minded leader requires that he

- is called as a Christian believer;
- is called to a leadership role and responsibilities;
- applies a biblical worldview as a leader;
- practices leadership according to a sound Christian ethic; and
- exercises leadership with technical knowledge, skill, and competence.

All of these requirements are needed. Being a faithful Christian is not sufficient for being an effective and ethical leader. A person also needs to master the skills and techniques that best support his leadership, adopting and seeking to apply models and practices and lessons from secular research. Since all truth is God's truth (Holmes 1984), a believer should be open to new leadership approaches, even those proposed and promoted by nonbelievers. If an innovative technique conforms to a biblical worldview or can be adapted to conform, a good leader might well consider applying it.

To be effective and ethical in a typical organizational setting, a leader should communicate a clear vision and purpose to followers. She also should demonstrate a sound moral character in honoring the rights of others while fulfilling her obligations in a principled, knowledgeable, and skillful manner. A Christian should be prepared to serve according to a sound biblical ethic, having studied to have a capability for ethical decision making and possessing the sanctified will to apply it. This requires attention to logical and sound thinking, application of the right principles for finding the truth, and acting with dedication. Above all, she should show love for God and for other people by using spiritually guided practical wisdom, seeking rational, sanctified reasons for what she thinks and does.

But is all this too idealistic? How can an ordinary mortal, even if truly called to faith and a leadership role, expect to succeed as a good leader, one who is not only ethical and effective but also spiritually directed? Trials and tribulations will arise to block one's way. Moreover, the world may appear to hate biblical obedience more than to admire or even tolerate it (1 John 3:13).

Seeking to avoid the temptations of the business world and workplace interaction with unbelievers, a Christian might establish or join a Christian organization. But this too may prove disappointing. Christian companies, colleges, charities, mission agencies, and local churches are social organizations employing humans, who all are imperfect in their spiritual sanctification, and some are tares who actually oppose God and his people (Matthew 13:38). Indeed, every human is a sinner (Romans 3:23, 1 John 1:8), subject to temptations to love himself and the things of the world, to lust, and to betray. Even a hermit in total social isolation lives with a sinner.

The leader seeking to be ethical and spiritual can look to other faithful people who can help and encourage. He can find people who will bless him in many ways. But the wise person must take great care choosing counselors —as some may be inadequate to the question at hand.

Furthermore, he might be disappointed to find that some people, even those in religious organizations, can backstab, deceive, and manipulate through decidedly unethical practices. Some justify their behavior pragmatically, believing good ends excuse any unethical means; others are unintentionally or intentionally ignorant in certain aspects of ethics; and some are hypocrites.

However, without trying to discern the motives of others, a spiritually minded leader needs to avoid being judgmental. Instead, he should humble himself, confess his own failings, and repent. Being called, a person's will is freed to choose to walk in faith, to confront trials without being tempted by God (James 1:13). And while this may seem surprising at times, keeping God's commandments is not burdensome (1 John 5:3). The leader can then be optimistic.

Developing into a good leader is indeed a great challenge. Making the correct choices and having the disposition to follow them ethically and spiritually, in spite of pressures to act otherwise, requires developed moral character strengths. Perfection is out of reach in this fallen world, but the person committed to develop his character can grow in virtue, when gracefully guided by the Holy Spirit. Whether or not he achieves financial wealth and fame in the world, he can become a good leader—a person who effectively carries the torch of leadership using ethically balanced means because he is spiritually endowed with the right character (reflecting a spiritually sanctified heart). A person called to lead thus can succeed, optimistically sharing God's exhortation to Joshua: "Have I not commanded you? Be strong and courageous! Do not tremble or be dismayed, for the LORD your God is with you wherever you go" (Joshua 1:9).

EXHIBIT 7
SOME IMPORTANT VIRTUES FOR A SPIRITUAL LEADER

Classical Greek Virtues	Christian Virtues (1 Corinthians 13:13)	Christian Moral Excellences (2 Peter 1:5-7)
Practical wisdom	Faith	Knowledge
Courage	Hope	Self-control
Temperance	Love	Perseverance
Justice	Godliness	Brotherly Kindness
		Love

Highly valued virtues in business leaders:

- Honesty, with technical competence (Whetstone 2001)
- Humility and professional will to succeed (Collins 2001)
- Practical Wisdom (Beabout 2012)

Questions for Discussion:

1. Consider some of the leaders you have known. If you rate some as better leaders than others, what do you think makes them better? Is it their superior technical leadership skills, their ethical commitment, or their moral character? Or is it some combination of these factors?

2. What particular character qualities or virtues do you believe you personally most need to be a good leader in your workplace? Do you think that working to develop these qualities will help or hinder your career advancement?

3. If you desire to develop the moral character of the good leader you believe you are called to be, what is your practical plan for doing so? Which of the practices suggested in this chapter do you intend to adopt?

4. Are you optimistic that you can develop as a good leader, one who is competent in leadership skills, ethical in conduct, and spiritually-minded? How will you measure your level of success? On Whom or what are you willing to place your trust for ultimate success?

APPENDIX

ESSAYS ON LEADERSHIP ISSUES

This book does not claim to cover all the many aspects of leadership. The informal essays in this appendix address several aspects or issues that students say are especially challenging for them. These include how to actually communicate a vision, the centrality and requirements of honesty and trust, how to delegate, the relevance of loyalty in today's business world, and when should a person quit his position. These issues are only representative of those that any leader can expect to confront. The essays hopefully will encourage discussion and raise practical concerns for leaders who must answer for themselves what practices are most appropriate in their particular organizational contexts and circumstances.

"COMMUNICATING A VISION"

Previously published in *Succeed to Lead*, 2:9
(November 2008) as "Communicating a Vision to
Your Organization."

C ommunicating vision is essential for effective leadership. A frequent quotation is, "Where there is no vision, the people perish (Proverbs 29:18a)." However, vision is not everything or even sufficient for good leadership. Ethicist Bowen McCoy notes that a vision without a plan is a hallucination. Indeed, when Proverbs 29:18 is fully quoted, it also qualifies the central importance of vision: "Where there is no vision, the people are unrestrained, but happy is he who keeps the law." A vision needs to be a good one, sought through a good plan. And the leader needs to communicate it well.

But how can he or she do so? I offer a case example I stumbled across in my research as I observed a company and its managers. The CEO's example provides a simple yet effective method for communicating a vision that any leader could emulate.

The hero of this case is the CEO of a chain of food stores in the Southeast US, which I will designate as GoodFood (not the real name). It was clear that this leader sought to run the most profitable stores in the region, maintaining a dominant market share, but also to do so in the right way. The company had no published code of ethics or vision statement; instead the CEO communicated a rather simple set of value priorities: the company and each employee should always (1) put God first, (2) put his family second, and (3) put the company and his job third.

This is not a new or unique set of priorities. Mary Kay and Coach Vince Lombardi espoused these value priorities, and so have many others. It was used by the CEO as the unifier toward the overall corporate objectives of profitability and ethical practice. It was his vision, one which he sought very deliberately and consistently to infuse into all management and employees.

As I observed GoodFood's operations, I was rather amazed to discover that almost all the store managers, other employees, and executives of this family-owned corporation actually knew the CEO's set of three priorities for the company and its employees. Indeed, more than one-third of those I interviewed actually volunteered this set of priorities or vision, even though I deliberately did not ask them about it. This is very unusual; studies typically find that employees, when asked, have little or no clue as to their CEO's or company's vision. When asked, employees often respond, "I don't think there is one," "I have no idea," or "I suppose it is to make money." At GoodFood, however, the employees did know the basic value priorities, and many shared this form of vision.

How did the food chain's managers, employees, and executives come to know the company's vision? Primarily, it was due to the diligence of the CEO. Every time he spoke to employees, met them individually in a store, met with staff and other executives, or spoke to external groups, civic clubs, or the media, he repeated his vision prioritizing God first, family second, and the company and job third. In the company, enculturation started with new employee orientation, when the CEO introduced the vision priorities in a video. The CEO repeated them so often, on seemingly every possible occasion, that one executive I interviewed complained about being dreadfully tired of hearing about them, that the CEO insisted on "going on and on about them at every meeting."

Store managers in Memphis and Little Rock said the CEO personally explained the GoodFood vision priorities to them when their stores were purchased from another firm. The CEO also "walks the talk" according to a manager with a long tenure in the company, explaining, "As long as the leader puts God first, you can be expected to be treated right and honestly, and you can trust and believe what is said to you." Another executive observed, "In this company, if the basic beliefs of the company weren't similar to yours, you couldn't stay here." Indeed, any significant value conflict in this strong culture would be unlikely as managers with opposing values tended to leave—or became rather convincing hypocrites.

The case of GoodFood and its CEO exemplifies a rather simple formula for communicating an organizational vision. The three basic components are:

1. Formulate a good vision, one that is purposeful, clear, and easy to understand. It must fit with the personal moral beliefs of the majority of the members of the organization.
2. The leader at the top must be committed to and consistently insist that planning is directed by the vision, and to live himself according to the vision. He must visibly "walk the talk" as a leader and as a person.
3. Repetition; the leaders at the top must constantly keep the vision before members of the organization.

This simple process succeeded well in GoodFood. Most of the executives, managers, and employees knew the vision set of value priorities, believed they were those of the CEO, and recognized the vision as a good, worthy one. Nor did the CEO let them forget it, repeating the vision statement at every possible opportunity.

But was this vision, or set of value priorities, the true or real ethic of GoodFood's culture? Time in the field suggested that many believed it was not. I detected greater skepticism among executives than at the store manager level. The major source of tension was financial pressures. When top management decided to cut costs, the easiest and quickest way was to cut labor expense, or jobs. A decision may be made at the top but it has to be administered through the chain of command. The villain in the eyes of the store manager or department manager may be the district manager, who in fact has simply been ordered to cut the budget. A store manager said, "Overall, [God first, family second, company third] are the company's values, but when they filter down..." An executive explained that the values of the vision fit his personal values, but people who have to get the job done can tend to be more short-term rather than long-term oriented. "The big openings [of new stores] kill people, run others off; we spend money on facilities rather than on people." Another executive was even more skeptical, "[The statement is] lip service... Sometimes I have to do things that I don't think are right but the company wants you to do them. But I will not compromise my morals for any amount of money. Of course I don't always see the whole picture."

Some managers also admitted that they personally struggled with the priorities. One commented, "My wife will say that I put God, work, and then family." GoodFood's vision priorities, while simple, easy to understand, and accepted as good ones, were not always easy to realize.

Nevertheless, working long and hard may be a good way to serve God and one's family, even if this requires more absence from church and family than one would prefer. Indeed, tension between potentially competing priorities can be a confirmation of their real existential meaning. Struggles or failures of managers and executives do not disprove the worth of those priorities nor the company's true desire to achieve them.

The case of GoodFood indeed shows that people within an organization can come to know and commit to a vision, and in spite of imperfections and doubts, accept it and seek to fulfill it. In GoodFood, the vision is not "window dressing" or a hallucination but a good and credible one. Such a vision can be communicated and established as a foundation of the organization's moral culture if

1. It is a good vision,
2. The organization's leaders are truly committed to plan according to the vision, and themselves live and promote the vision, and
3. This vision is repeated continually to stress its reality and importance.

"HONESTY AND TRUST"

(previously published in *Succeed to Lead*, 2:5; April 2008)

*H*onesty is an essential virtue for ethical business activity, perhaps the most important in most organizational cultures. In the Aristotelian sense, it is properly a golden mean between the vice manifest in chronic deception, lying, and misrepresentation and the opposing vice of untactful naivety, total honesty projected without reasonable and sensible restraint. Empirical research (Whetstone 2003) ranks honesty as the highest of the required manager virtues in a grocery chain, whereas the dishonest manager is considered the worst, most vicious, of all. The related virtue of trust is also highly rated, widely acclaimed as being essential for right and good ethics. Archie Carroll (2009, 110) says trust is the one characteristic that is crucial to leadership application, no matter the people involved, the circumstances or the situation. Businesses are built on a foundation of trust in the free-enterprise system (Richardson and McCord 2004); thus trust is also an essential attribute of an ethical organizational culture. Lack of trust is dysfunctional for the team, the firm, and the economic system.

However, there is a deep, darker side of the relationship value of trust. Trust involves *telos*, a sense of mutual agreement on purpose or ends, together with a working consensus on the means and practices guiding behaviors. This is good on a prima facie basis, but mutual agreement, even when reached, may not always be directed toward a good end or goal. Trust is instrumentally necessary for a gang of thieves as well as for a coterie of angels. Even when the intended end is accepted by all, there may be significant differences regarding acceptable means. For example a college faculty might agree that improving student retention is critically important but disagree with the administration that going softer on grading is the way to accomplish this end.

Because of the need to establish and maintain trust, a leader needs subordinates to share his or her basic view of the appropriate manner of conduct for their respective assignments. A pragmatic, goal-oriented leader might trust more the subordinate who will go along than one who out of religious or other moral principles might have qualms or objections to what the leader believes is necessary for the job. Ethical integrity in the superior-subordinate relationship is fostered when the subordinate has the personal integrity and the relational support to question or even challenge the boss (Follett 1987), rather than when honing to "whatever the boss says is right" (essentially the Nuremburg defense). For his part, the leader should refrain from "the thirty thousand foot defense" recently attributed to former Enron and Worldcom Chairmen/CEOs claiming they were too far above the day-to-day actions of their subordinates and thus not responsible for their unethical or illegal acts.

A pragmatic, goal-oriented leader might sooner trust the subordinate who loyally "goes along" rather than the one who raises objections to what the leader believes is needed for the task at hand. Even if the leader recognizes and basically respects the religious or other principled source of the latter, are the likely frictions necessary or even acceptable? A strong transformational leader may even have difficulty recognizing or assessing the need for constraints that problematic naysayers represent. Indeed, why should a goal-focused leader rely upon or even employ a strongly principle-focused subordinate in a close working relationship? For example, when hiring a personal assistant, would not such a leader choose the more amenable applicant, the one who can be most trusted for personal loyalty, rather than the principled applicant, the one who might raise uncomfortable questions concerning the means the leader deems most expedient for succeeding in his personal and corporate agendas? Is there perhaps some hiring bias against the principled candidate?

"DELEGATION"

(previously published in *Succeed to Lead*, 3:14,
August 2009, as "A Fundamental Leadership Principle —
Why Not Follow It?")

A good leader should delegate authority and responsibility equally, while retaining ultimate accountability. This is a fundamental principle: the good leader ensures that a follower assigned a responsibility for a task, large or small, is also given the administrative, resource, information, and other required operational support—and the genuine authority within the organization—needed for successful achievement of the task. Too much authority is unnecessary and might lead to counterproductive abuses of power. Too little authority puts unfair pressure on the person given the responsibility, hindering her ability to succeed. Authority and responsibility need to be equal.

This rather simple principle goes back not only to Henri Fayol, the father of modern management theory, but to the dawn of time. Most basically, it is a matter of common sense and fairness. However, why don't we follow it? My management and leadership students admit they are poor delegators. They know the principle and are convinced it is correct, and that it works. This is why many identify their chronic inability to delegate and empower properly as their greatest, and personally most troubling, weakness as a practicing leader. In turn, we can be frustrated by our leader's weakness in delegating. As an experienced academic department chairperson responsible for overseeing the design, development, and offering of a course curriculum for educating college students, I am hindered when administrators micromanage instead of allowing me to administer the policies and solve the problems that arise. You can think of other examples from your own experience. Perhaps you are one of the fortunate few who have not been given some job responsibility by a superior without the appropriate degree of authority. But, perhaps not.

You might be able to recall some positive examples, as well. One comes from God, who knows this delegation principle and in His perfection exemplifies it. The New Testament gives the history of God's strategy for starting and prospering the Christian Church. God laid the foundation in the redemptive sacrificial work of Christ on the cross. He then delegated the responsibility for establishing His church to men called to take the gracious gospel of Jesus Christ throughout the world.

> And Jesus came up and spoke to them, saying, "All authority has been given to Me in heaven and on earth. Go therefore and make disciples of all the nations, baptizing them in the name of the Father and the Son and the Holy Spirit, teaching them to observe all that I commanded you; and lo, I am with you always, even to the end of the age." (Matthew 28:18-20; also see Mark 16:15-20)

The ignorant, sinful, and fearful eleven remaining disciples had been trained for their future responsibilities, but they knew they were not up to this great task. God chose to empower them with the Holy Spirit (Luke 24:49). God did not shield them from difficulty, hardship, and death (John 21:17-19) in carrying out their responsibility, nor did He micromanage. God chose not to reveal all the details of His plan although He intervened to provide guidance at critical times (for examples, see Acts 9 and 16:6-10). Although empowered with the mind of Christ, the apostles and other witnesses and future martyrs still had to exercise their free wills in deciding what to do and where to go, being free to differ over tactics, disagree with one another, make mistakes, and submit to various temptations. They were not made into superheroes, at least not in the comic book sense. But being made new creations in Christ and accompanied by the ever present Spirit of Christ, they were given enough authority and genuinely empowered (see Titus 2:15) to the degree needed to meet their assigned responsibilities magnificently. Because of the extraordinary nature of the task, the Holy Spirit provided Christ's representatives with healing and other miraculous powers, to the extent needed to confirm their authority. These men and women were not overly exalted, however, but succeeded when they acted in proper humility (Luke 10:17-20). God remained in sovereign control, and thus ultimately accountable, but He chose to use mortal men and women by delegating the right amount of authority and responsibility (in equivalent proportions).

This was not an innovative leadership approach. God showed the proper way to delegate from the very beginning in his original Creation account (Genesis 1:27-28). He delegated great authority to humans over all of creation, although limited by one negative command (Genesis 2:15-17). He did not choose to micromanage, but allowed men and women the free will to choose and act, even if the result were to prove disastrous, as indeed it did, leading to the fall. As the perfect, compassionate, and gracious ruler, God would rectify the errors of his subordinates through the redeeming work of Jesus Christ. But as a leader, He did not intervene with man's operational decisions, even though He had the power to do so and could foresee the consequences of man's incorrect choices.

Nor is the principle of proper delegation just for Christians. It is a creation ordinance, something that works well for all people in various social organizations. For example, we can learn from the example of the Egyptian Pharaoh who put Joseph over all the land of Egypt, subject only to his own power of the throne (Genesis 41:39-42). Pharaoh knew how to delegate.

Are you a good enough leader to learn and apply this lesson? We are not perfect and cannot expect to be perfect leaders. But the best way to lead is by delegating properly, assigning responsibilities, and empowering with the corresponding adequate level of authority. Moreover, we need to retain the ultimate accountability to accept blame for our subordinates' lapses and to award them the praise and recognition, even in those cases when we have had to make some repairs. Are we good enough leaders to follow the fundamental principle of delegation?

"LOYALTY"

(previously published in *Succeed to Lead*, 3:13,
June 2009, as "Is Loyalty Still a Business Virtue?")

L oyalty is one of those old-fashioned virtues that no longer make much sense to today's practical leaders. Movers and shakers seem to believe that companies can no longer be truly loyal, and neither can employees. Top corporate leaders and even the academic administrations of Christian institutions often view individual employees instrumentally, as being worthy only in terms of the incremental contribution they make.

Is loyalty really out of date? Only if one is self-autonomous. However, leader-follower and employer-employee relationships are two-way commitments. They do not have to be between those equal in power and status. Indeed the loyalty involved in God's covenant is not between equals, but is still vital for the believer in spiritual union with Christ.

Loyalty among humans has limits because of the competing objects of one's loyalty. Being totally loyal to one person can lead to lack of loyalty toward others. A husband vows to be ever loyal to his wife and vice versa; adulterous behavior by either party breaks the vow and damages the relationship. This may lead to morally justified actions, even divorce. A loyal employee may be faced with choosing to blow the whistle against his employer when the latter leads the organization unethically, such as harming the environment, customers, employees, owners or other stakeholders unlawfully or contrary to the organization's mission. The whistleblower can be deemed disloyal and thus be persecuted by his superiors and coworkers. But the whistleblower may be acting out of a sense of loyalty that contradicts his loyalty to his superiors. Scripture directs Christians to obey their earthly masters in all things with sincerity of heart (Colossians 3:22) but also teaches one to obey God rather than men (Acts 5:29). The Christian at work will have to decide if his ethic can be, "Whatever my boss says, is right, and I will do it." Obedience depends on what the "it" is.

Leadership requires one to prioritize or balance loyalties. Should one stay late at work to help a coworker complete a key organizational task, risking the wrath of his spouse? Should his boss encourage or even allow this? The best answer is not always evident, requiring the employee and the leader to examine their worldview-directed moral compasses, appealing with moral imagination to their full set of virtues, responsibilities, and the greater good.

C. S. Lewis seems to mock loyalty when he portrays the Dufflepuds in *The Voyage of the Dawn Treader*. These creatures, in their silliness, are extremely loyal to their incompetent leader, affirming all he says:

> "Well done, Chief. You never said a truer word. You never made a better plan, Chief. You couldn't have a better plan than that... Couldn't have a better order. Just what we were going to say ourselves. Off we go!" (1970, 112-13)

This attitude indeed is rather silly, though perhaps not far from that of the faculties and staffs that Lewis may have been mocking. Since even the ethical Christian has stewardship responsibilities in a real world, she must be practical rather than blindly loyal. One must keep her resume current and stay flexible enough to move to another job at any favorable opportunity.

Loyalty as a virtue involves much more than being a "yes man" like the Dufflepuds. Peter Drucker (1967, 148) said that Alfred P. Sloan, the man who led General Motors into becoming the world's largest manufacturing enterprise, once addressed this phenomenon at a committee meeting: "Gentlemen, I take it we are all in complete agreement on the decision here." Everyone around the table nodded assent. "Then," continued Mr. Sloan, "I propose we postpone further discussion of this matter until our next meeting to give ourselves time to develop disagreement and perhaps gain some understanding of what the decision is all about."

Early management researcher Mary Parker Follett stressed that followers are vital for helping the leader understand the situation and control it. The leader needs a genuine open-door policy to provide the leader the information and criticism that she must have. This requires continual effort to maintain a relationship of trust and respect, as is of course due among all God-imagers. However, one must be careful not to go too far, earning the label of "confrontational junkie" by appearing to enjoy the battle even more than winning it. By working to create and fuel conflict rather than to resolve it constructively, confrontational junkies are not truly loyal to their superiors, though at the extreme opposite of Dufflepuds. The leader and followers need to seek a virtuous middle ground or Golden Mean by working to build an ethical and effective team consensus.

To avoid the detriments of groupthink, however, the leader must guard against the natural tendency of being overly defensive. He should encourage rather than punish those who are willing to share legitimate concerns. Whereas the ideas of the team player and the power of positive thinking (Blanchard and Peale 1988) sometimes are perceived to mean that a positive, reliably loyal employee never objects, a truly loyal follower may at times have to exercise the courage to stand up for what he understands is right. Is this disloyal or does it represent a higher loyalty? This requires tolerating some dissent, even if uncomfortable. Good ideas need to be challenged, bad ideas even more so. If the group makes a decision with which the follower still cannot agree, one should seek to learn from it and move ahead to the next decision, as allowed by conscience (McCoy 2007). This approach is not relativistic although it requires humility in the midst of complexity.

While few leaders and employees act as extreme Dufflepuds or confrontational junkies, it can be difficult to find the virtuous mean. Nevertheless, one can do so. Jack, senior vice president for corporate planning for a Fortune 500 corporation, worked many years to find the right merger candidate to achieve the diversification he sincerely believed the company needed. But the Chairman/CEO would never agree to any target company proposed to him. After retiring, the former chairman became terminally ill. Jack, upon visiting him in the hospital, was surprised by his former boss's greeting, "Hello, Jack, faithful to the end." After some thought, Jack realized that his former boss knew something that he had thought was a deep secret. Years before, several other company top executives decided to force the chairman's retirement, believing that he would never approve the major acquisition that they thought necessary. These executives went to Jack to invite him to join their conspiracy. But Jack immediately refused, asking to be counted out of their group. The executives soon abandoned their efforts and nothing was ever said about it again, at least to Jack's knowledge. The dying former chairman indicated to Jack that he did learn of the conspiracy and Jack's loyalty to him rather than to his own career interests in consummating an acquisition. Jack passed the loyalty test and was blessed with a foretaste of the declaration each Christian leader should desire from his ultimate boss, Jesus Christ: "Well done, good and faithful servant."

"WHEN SHOULD YOU QUIT?"

(previously published in *Succeed to Lead*, 2:8, October 2008)

*I*f you have never considered quitting your job (without another offer in sight), either you are brand new, have a rather flabby moral compass, or are magnificently and unusually blessed. Most jobs, regardless of field, can be frustrating and tiresome from time-to-time, even when a person is content within her true calling. Bosses, coworkers, subordinates, customers, suppliers, and government regulators can be stumbling blocks and infuriating, at least occasionally, given the fallen world and the sinfulness of people. Sometimes, due to our mistakes or to events beyond our control, our plans and programs can disappoint, even fail. One may even be asked to do something he deems unethical. But don't think too quickly about quitting.

Winston Churchill, a leader who had numerous failures, often disastrous ones, taught that the good leader is one who fails and learns from his failures, continuing at the mission until he finds success. He was not a quitter.

However, when is it right to quit?

Robert E. Lee chose to surrender to Ulysses Grant at Appomattox in April 1865, even though Lee's men pleaded with him to fight on. Confederate president Jefferson Davis refused to quit and fled Virginia to join Joe Johnston's army of Tennessee, urging them to fight on for the Confederate cause. Is there sometimes virtue in quitting?

Hillary Clinton refused to quit her campaign for the Democratic presidential nomination until the late August 2008 convention, even though Barack Obama had secured the required votes long before. Mitt Romney had long prior abandoned his campaign for the Republican nomination after John McCain built a strong lead. Richard Nixon resigned when threatened with impeachment over Watergate. Bill Clinton, under impeachment proceedings in Congress, refused to resign. The political and social circumstances as well as particulars of cases vary, so deciding to quit or not can be difficult. One's moral compass matters, but in which direction does it point?

This can be an issue for any manager or employee. What should the employee do when asked by his manager to act in a manner contrary to his ethical beliefs, such as to hide potentially damning evidence, to overestimate the capabilities of the company's products, or to hire someone he feels is under qualified? Is the employee caught between the "Scylla" of quitting and the "Charybdis" of going along in moral compromise?

Sometimes perhaps, but Joanne Ciulla (1991) affirms that the really creative part of ethics is refusing to do either. Instead, develop other alternatives, ones that can enable the organization to meet its objectives in ways that are ethically acceptable. For example, perhaps the employee can persuade the manager that it would be better to "come clean" and move on, or to promote other aspects of one's product, possibly to a different market, or to suggest another, more suitable position for the person the manager wants along with a superior person for the original position. These alternatives may not always be accepted, but the truly creative and dedicated employee can continue to search for others. He may convince his manager, or at least stimulate him to be more creative and ethical. If not, and the ethical battle appears lost, then the employee can reconsider his position. If he resigns, he at least has not done so prematurely or rashly. This can lead to the next question, which also rates careful consideration.

Should a Person Who Quits because of the Manager Reveal His Real Reason for Leaving?

Jeffrey Seglin (2005) tells of a reader who got a call from his son-in-law asking for advice after quitting his position with two weeks' notice. He left because of his supervisor, whom he considered to be a poor manager. When the quitting employee gave notice, his supervisor asked him to meet to offer an evaluation of her, particularly of her management style. The employee was concerned about insulting her and jeopardizing the goodwill he had built.

The father-in-law advised, "Lie! Tell her she's not the reason you're leaving. Just tell her you're leaving because of a salary hike and a new opportunity, which you find exciting. It is not your responsibility to straighten out that company or that person. Let her superiors figure it out."

Did the father-in-law give the right advice? Seglin answers that he was right to advise his son-in-law to consider his best interests. This is prudent: one may have to depend on a former supervisor for a future job reference. He should take care and avoid engaging in a gripe session. He definitely should not insult her by openly saying, "You're terrible and here's why."

However, that doesn't mean he should lie—or violate his worldview in any way. If he does, he will leave his former colleagues working for a boss who will continue to think that she is doing well. Instead, the son-in-law can use that hour with his former boss to offer constructive responses to any questions she might have about her management style. If he does not answer frankly, the deficient boss might not soon, if ever, learn what she needs to correct. Sometimes a supervisor keeps or even promotes an inadequate manager because he presents no threat to her own position. "Normally, a boob has a boob for a boss," says Angelo Calvello, a principal at a financial firm in Chicago. The "boobs" often become political allies in disguising their mutual incompetence (Sandberg 2005).

Often incompetent managers are retained because the people who hired or promoted them are reluctant to admit they made an error. Sometimes they acted without seeking the advice of more knowledgeable subordinates; acknowledging their error is an affront to their egos. This has been consistent with human weakness ever since the Fall.

Returning to the young man considering the advice of his father-in-law, if he truly believes some good might come from his sit-down discussion with his boss, he would be right in offering constructive comments and criticisms. He should avoid challenging her too negatively, but rather tactfully focus on things that might result in her rethinking the way she approaches her employees. This would cultivate the possibility, however remote, of planting seeds that lead to improved conditions for the colleagues he leaves behind and for the supervisor's growth as well. Moreover, this is the more ethical, worldview grounded approach, although perhaps a supererogatory one requiring courage beyond the call of duty.

However, it is wise to be very careful in reporting one's supervisor to his superior. The subordinate is not only lower in rank, he often has an incomplete perspective as to what has really been transpiring. The following is anecdotal, but revealing nevertheless. In the course of interviewing a young woman in England as to her work experience and values, she described her experience working in a manufacturing facility with other women employees. The supervisor of these women was rumored to be having an affair during work hours with a man who worked elsewhere in the plant. This was affecting morale and productivity, due to the supervisor's absence at critical times and the disruptions due to rampant gossiping. In the interview, the young woman said that she finally decided to report the supervisor and the rumors to the plant manager. Afterward, the supervisor started to make life miserable for all the workers in her charge. After quitting, the young woman whom I interviewed found out the truth—the supervisor was conducting the affair with the plant manager himself. Reporting the rumor to him did not solve the problem, at least in this case.

The above examples address the Christian's character commitment to be loyal and how he might best address the difficult decision of quitting his job. It can help to consider such unpleasant choices objectively, before we find that we must. A leader will face many more issues, ones for which he will be wise to prepare. (For additional common grace decision-making insights, see Tichy and Bennis 2007.) The choices the leader makes in his free will are ultimately grounded in his actual worldview, which may differ from the one he hopes to follow. A spiritually minded, ethical leader will ultimately succeed if, as the Psalmist, he can sincerely say, "I would rather stand at the threshold of the house of my God, than dwell in the tents of wickedness" (Psalm 84:10b).

REFERENCES

Adams, S. 2010. "The Perfect Stimulus: Bad Management." *Wall Street Journal*, November 6-7, C3.

Aeschliman, M. D. 2007. "Virtue's Aristocrat." *National Review*, April 2, 46-47, 51.

Alzola, M. 2012. "The Possibility of Virtue." *Business Ethics Quarterly* 22 (2): 377-404.

Ambrose, S. 1992. *Band of Brothers, E Company, 506th Regiment, 101st Airborne: From Normandy to Hitler's Eagle's Nest*. NY: Simon & Schuster.

Anderson, C. 2004. "Dick Winters: Reflections on the Band of Brothers, D-Day, and Leadership" (interview). *American History*.

Anderson, D. 1993. "Lost and Found." *National Review*, November 15, 58-60.

Anscombe, E. 1958. "Modern Moral Philosophy." *Philosophy* 33: 1-19.

Aquinas, T. n.d. "Treatise on Law." *Summa Theologica, Questions 90-97*. Chicago: Henry Regenery.

Aristotle. 1976. *The Nicomachean Ethics*. Translated by J. Thomson. Revised with note and appendices by H. Tredennick. Introduction and bibliography by J. Barnes. London: Penguin.

Avolio, B. J. and W. L. Gardner. 2005. "Authentic Leadership Development: Getting to the Root of Positive Forms of Leadership." *Leadership Quarterly* 16(3): 315-38.

Banks, R., and B. Ledbetter. 2004. *Reviewing Leadership: A Christian Evaluation of Current Approaches.* Grand Rapids, MI: Baker.

Barnett, T. "Spirituality in Leadership." *Reference for Business. Encyclopedia of Business,* 2nd ed., 1-6. Accessed November 29, 2010, at http:www.referenceforbusiness.com/management/Sc-Str/Spirituality-in-Leadership.html.

Basil. 1965. *Aux jeunes gens sur la maniere de tirer des lettres Helleniques.* Paris: Societe d'Edition "Les Belles Lettres," I, quoted in Kelly (2008, 211).

Bass, B. 1990. *Bass and Stogdill's Handbook of Leadership: Theory, Research, and Managerial Applications,* 3rd ed. New York: Free Press.

Bass, B., and P. Steidlmeier. 2004. "Ethics, Character, and Authentic Transformational Leadership Behavior." *Ethics: The Heart of Leadership,* 2nd ed. Edited by J. Ciulla. Westport, CT: Praeger, 175-96.

Beabout, J. 2012. "Management as a Domain-Relative Practice That Requires and Develops Practical Wisdom." *Business Ethics Quarterly* 22 (2): 405-32.

Bellah, R., R. Madsen, et al. 1985. *Habits of the Heart.* Berkeley, CA: University of California Press.

Bennett, W. J. 1993. *The Book of Virtues: A Treasury of Great Moral Stories.* New York: Simon & Schuster.

Birzer, B. 2012. "Making Modernity Human: Can Christian Humanism Redeem an Age of Ideology?" *The American Conservative* 11 (8): August, 40-42.

Blake, R., and A. McCanse. 1991. *Leadership Dilemmas-Grid Solutions.* Houston, TX: Gulf.

Blake, R., and J. Mouton. 1985. *The Managerial Grid III.* Houston, TX: Gulf.

Blamires, H. 1978. *The Christian Mind: How Should a Christian Think?* Ann Arbor, MI: Servant Books.

Blanchard, K., and N. V. Peale. 1988. *The Power of Ethical Management.* New York: Morrow.

Block, Peter. 1987. *The Empowered Manager.* San Francisco: Jossey-Bass.

Bowie, N. 2000. "Business Ethics, Philosophy, and the Next Twenty-Five Years." *Business Ethics Quarterly* 10 (1): 7-20.

Brady, F. N. 1990. *Ethical Managing: Rules and Results.* New York: Macmillan.

Brawley, R., ed. 2007. *Character Ethics and the New Testament: Moral Dimensions of Scripture.* Louisville, KY: Westminster John Knox.

Briner, B. 1997. *The Leadership Lessons of Jesus: A Timeless Model for Today's Leaders.* Nashville, TN: Broadman & Holman.

Burns, J. M. 1978. *Leadership.* New York: Harper & Row.

Butler, Joseph. 1726. "Upon Self-Deceit: Fifteen Sermons upon Human Nature." *Vice and Virtue in Everyday Life: Introductory Readings in Ethics,* 5th ed. Christina Sommers and Fred Sommers (2001). Fort Worth, TX: Harcourt College Publishers, 397-403.

Cadbury, H. 1962. *The Peril of Modernizing Jesus.* London: SPCK.

Calvin, J. n.d. *Institutes of the Christian Religion.* Translated by Ford Lewis Battles. Edited and introduced by John T. McNeill. (1960). The Library of Christian Classics 20-21. Philadelphia, PA: The Westminster Press.

Calvin, J. n.d. *Letters* 1 (213).

Carr, A. 1968. "Is Business Bluffing Ethical?" *Harvard Business Review* 46, January/February.

Carroll, A. 2009. *Business Ethics: Brief Readings on Vital Topics.* New York and London: Routledge.

Carter, L. E. Sr. 2007. "Global Ethical Leadership and Higher Education: 'Being the Change You Wish to See'." *For the Common Good: The Ethics of Leadership in the Twenty-First Century.* Edited by J. Knapp. Westport, CT: Praeger, 137-49.

Chappell, T. 1993. *The Soul of a Business: Managing for Profit and the Common Good.* New York: Bantam.

Chewning, R. C., ed. 1989. *Biblical Principles and Business: The Foundations.* Colorado Springs, CO: Navpress.

Chewning, R., J. Eby, and S. Roels. 1990. *Business through the Eyes of Faith.* San Francisco: Harper & Row.

Ciulla, J. B. 1991. "Business Ethics as Moral Imagination." *Business Ethics: The State of the Art.* Edited by R. E. Freeman. New York: Oxford University Press.

Ciulla, J. B. 2004. *Ethics: The Heart of Leadership,* 2nd ed. Westport, CT: Praeger.

Ciulla, J. B. 2005. "The State of Leadership Ethics and the Work That Lies before Us." *Business Ethics: A European Review* 14 (4): 323-35.

Ciulla, J. B. 2006. "Ethics: The Heart of Leadership." *Responsible Leadership.* Edited by T. Maak and N. M. Pless. London: Routledge, 17-32.

Coenen, L. 1975. "Call." *The New International Dictionary of New Testament Theology.* Edited by C. Brown. Grand Rapids, MI: Zondervan, 271-76.

Cohen, N. H. 1995. *Mentoring Adult Learners: A Guide for Educators and Trainers*. Malabar, FL: Krieger.

Collins, J. 2001. *Good to Great*. New York: HarperCollins.

Cone, J. 1969. *Black Theology and Black Power*. New York: Seabury.

Crocker, H. 1999. *Robert E. Lee on Leadership*. Rocklin, CA: Prima.

Crockett, W. 1976. "How to Be a Good Follower." *Industry Week*. November 15.

Curtis, E. M. 2000. *Transformed Thinking: Loving God with All Your Mind*. Franklin, TN: JKO.

Deal, T., and A. Kennedy. 1982. *Corporate Culture: The Rites and Rituals of Corporate Life*. Reading, PA: Addison-Wesley.

DeGraff, D., C. Tilley, and L. Neal. 2001. *Servant-Leadership Characteristics in Organizational Life*. The Greenleaf Center for Servant-Leadership. Monograph Booklet 6.

De Jong, Norman. 2001. *Teaching for a Change: A Transformational Approach to Education*. Phillipsburg, NJ: P & R Publishing.

Derry, R. 1991. "Institutionalizing Ethical Motivation: Reflections on Goodpaster's Agenda." *Business Ethics: The State of the Art*. Edited by E. Freeman. New York: Oxford University Press.

Didache. 1970. *Early Church Fathers*. Edited by C. C. Richardson. New York: Macmillan.

Donaldson, T., and R. E. Freeman, eds. 1994. *Business as a Humanity*. New York: Oxford University Press.

Doris, J. M. 1998. "Persons, Situations, and Virtue Ethics." *Nous* 32: 504-30.

Dorr, D. 2008. "Alternative Business Ethics: A Challenge for Leadership." *Leadership and Business Ethics.* Edited by G. Flynn. Dordrecht: Springer, 211-27.

Drucker, P. F. 1967. *The Effective Executive.* New York: Harper & Row.

Duska, R., and J. A. Ragatz. 2008. "How Losing Soul Leads to Ethical Corruption in Business," in *Leadership and Business Ethics.* Edited by G. Flynn. Dordrecht: Springer, 151-63.

Fayol, H. 1916. *General and Industrial Management.* Translated by C. Storrs. London: Pitman.

Ferry, L. 2011. *A Brief History of Thought: A Philosophical Guide to Living.* New York: Harper Perennial.

Fiedler, F. 1967. *A Theory of Leadership Effectiveness.* New York: McGraw-Hill.

Finley, A. 2010. "The Weekend Interview with James Watson: A Geneticist's Cancer Crusade." *Wall Street Journal,* November 27-28, A15.

Flanagan, O. 1991. *Varieties of Moral Personality: Ethics and Psychological Realism.* Cambridge, MA: Harvard University Press.

Fletcher, J. 1966. *Situation Ethics.* Philadelphia: The Westminster Press.

Fluker, W. "Spirituality, Ethics, and Leadership." *Spirituality in Higher Education* Newsletter 4 (3): June 2008, 1-6.

Flynn, G., ed. 2008. "The Virtuous Manager: A Vision for Leadership in Business." *Leadership and Business Ethics.* Dordrecht: Springer, 39-56.

Flynn, G., and P. H. Werhane. 2008. "Introduction." *Leadership and Business Ethics.* Edited by G. Flynn. Dordrecht: Springer, 1-12.

Follett, M. P. 1924. *Creative Experience.* Boston: Longmans, Green, and Company.

Follett, M. P. 1987. "The Essentials of Leadership." *The Great Writings in Management and Organizational Behavior,* 2nd ed. Edited by L. Boone and D. Bowen. New York: Random House.

Foot, P. 1978. *Virtues and Vices and Other Essays in Moral Philosophy.* Oxford: Basil Blackwell.

Ford, L. 1991. *Jesus: The Transforming Leader.* London: Hodder & Stoughton.

Fortin, J. 2006. *The Centered Life.* Minneapolis, MN: Augsburg Fortress.

Fowler, J. W. 1981. *Stages of Faith: The Psychology of Human Development and the Quest for Meaning.* New York: Harper & Row.

Fry, L. W. 2003. "Toward a Theory of Spiritual Leadership." *Leadership Quarterly* 14 (6): 693-727.

Gariepy, H. 1991. "Nehemiah: God's Man of Action-2." *The War Cry,* February 16, 9.

Garofalo Neto, E. 2011. "The Soccer World Cup 2010 as a Sub-Creation: An Analysis of Human Play through a Theological Grid of Creation-Fall-Redemption" (unpublished PhD dissertation). Jackson, MS: Reformed Theological Seminary.

Gelfand, M., V. Major, J. Raver, L. Nishii, and K. O'Brien. 2007. "Negotiating Relationally: The Dynamics of the Relational Self in Negotiations." *Academy of Management Review* 31 (2): 427-51.

George, B. 2003. *Authentic Leadership: Rediscovering the Secrets to Creating Lasting Value.* San Francisco: Jossey-Bass.

Gilder, George. 1993. *Wealth and Poverty.* San Francisco: ICS Press.

Goldman, S. 2011. "Dawn of the Idols." *The American Conservative,* June, 44-46.

Goleman, D. 2004. "What Makes a Leader?" *Harvard Business Review*, January, 82-91.

Graham, J. W. 1991. "Servant Leadership in Organizations: Inspirational and Moral." *Leadership Quarterly* 2 (2): 105-19.

Greenleaf, R. K. 1977. *Servant Leadership: A Journey into the Nature of Legitimate Power and Greatness*. New York: Paulist Press.

Griffiths, B. 2005. "The Business of Values." *The Heart of a Business Ethic*. Edited by D. Holt. With an introduction and afterword by W. C. Pollard and a foreword by W. Bennis. Lanham, MD: University Press of America, 32-56.

Grint, K. 2000. *The Arts of Leadership*. Oxford, UK: Oxford University Press.

Gustafson, J. 1971. *Christian Ethics and the Community*. Philadelphia: Pilgrims Press.

Handy, C. 1999. *The Hungry Spirit*. Broadway Books.

Harkness, G. 1931. *John Calvin: The Man and His Ethics*. Nashville: Abingdon.

Harman, G. 1999. "Moral Philosophy Meets Social Psychology: Virtue Ethics and the Fundamental Attribution Error." *Proceedings of the Aristotelian Society* 99: 315-31.

Harper, N. E. 1981. *Making Disciples: The Challenge of Christian Education at the End of the Twentieth Century*. Jackson, MS: Reformed Theological Seminary.

Harrison, J., and C. St. John. 2010. *Foundations in Strategic Management*, 5th ed. Mason, OH: South-Western Cengage Learning.

Hartman, E. M. 2008. "Socratic Questions and Aristotelian Answers: A Virtue-Based Approach to Business Ethics." *Leadership and Business Ethics.* Edited by G. Flynn. Dordrecht: Springer, 81-101.

Hauerwas, S. 1974. *Vision and Virtue: Essays in Christian Ethical Reflections.* Notre Dame, IN: Fide.

Hazony, Y. 2012. *The Philosophy of Hebrew Scripture.* Cambridge, UK: Cambridge University Press.

Heiges, D. R. 1984. *The Christian's Calling.* Philadelphia: Fortress.

Hesse, H. 1956. *The Journey to the East.* New York: The Noonday Press.

Hill, Bennett D. 1990. "Benedict Writes his Monastic Rule." *Christian History* 28: 17-18.

Hodge, C. 1857. *An Exposition of the First Epistle to the Corinthians,* reprint ed. Robert Carter and Brothers (1980). Grand Rapids, MI: Baker.

Holmes, A. F. 1983. *Contours of a Worldview.* Grand Rapids, MI: Eerdmans.

Holmes, A. F. 1984. *Ethics: Approaching Moral Decisions.* Downers Grove, IL: InterVarsity.

House, R. J., P. J. Hanges, M. Javidan, P. W. Dorfman, and V. Gupta, eds. 2004. *Culture, Leadership, and Organizations: The GLOBE Study of 62 Societies.* Thousand Oaks, CA: Sage.

House, R., and T. Mitchell. 1974. "Path-Goal Theory of Leadership." *Contemporary Business* (Fall): 81-98.

Huff, C., L. Barnard, and W. Frey. 2008. "Good Computing: A Pedagogically Focused Model of Virtue in the Practice of Computing, Parts I & II." *Journal of Communication and Ethics in Society* 6 (3): 246-78, and 6 (4): 284-316.

Iwata, E. 1995. "Some Executives Are Trying to Make Companies Heed a Higher Authority." *Reflections on Leadership*. Edited by L. Spears. New York: John Wiley & Sons, 126-28.

Jennings, M. M. 2006. "Tylenol: The Product and Its Packaging Safety." *Business Ethics: Case Studies and Selected Readings*, 5th ed. Mason, OH: Thomson/Southwestern, 503-5.

Johann, R. 1968. *Building the Human*. New York: Herder and Herder.

Johnson, C. 2001. *Meeting the Ethical Challenges of Leadership*. Thousand Oaks, CA: Sage.

Johnson, P. 2003. "An 'Ism' for All Seasons." *National Review*, October 13.

Jones, L. B. 1995. *Jesus CEO: Using Ancient Wisdom for Visionary Leadership*. New York: Hyperion.

Josephson, M. 1988. "Teaching Ethical Decision Making and Principled Reasoning." *Ethics: Easier Said Than Done* 1: 27-33.

Judge, T., R. Illies, J. Bono, and M. Gerhardt. 2002. "Personality and Leadership: A Qualitative and Quantitative Review." *Journal of Applied Psychology* 87 (4): 765-68.

Jung, D., and J. Sosik. 2006. "Who Are the Spellbinders? Identifying Personal Attributes of Charismatic Leaders." *Journal of Leadership and Organizational Studies* 12: 12-26.

Kaplan, S. N., M. M. Klebanov, and M. Sorensen. "Which CEO Characteristics and Abilities Matter?" *Swedish Institute for Financial Research Conference on the Economics of the Private Equity Market: AFA 2008 New Orleans Meeting Paper*. Accessed at SSRN:http://ssrn.com/abstract=972446.

Keeley, M. 1995. "The Trouble with Transformational Leadership: Toward a Federalist Ethic for Organizations." *Business Ethics Quarterly* 5 (1): 67-96.

Kelley, R. 1992. *The Power of Followership*. New York: Doubleday/ Currency.

Kelly, D. F. 2008. *Systematic Theology, Vol. I: The God Who Is: The Holy Trinity*. Fearn, Ross-Hire, Scotland, UK: Christian Focus.

Kempis, T. A. 1965. *The Imitation of Christ*. Edited by P. S. McElroy. Mount Vernon, NY: Peter Pauper.

Kiechel, W. 1995. "The Leader as Servant." *Reflections on Leadership*. Edited by L. Spears. New York: John Wiley & Sons, 121-25.

Knapp, J., ed. 2007. *For the Common Good: The Ethics of Leadership in the Twenty-First Century*. Westport, CT: Praeger.

Kouzes, J., and B. Posner, eds. 2004. *Christian Reflections on the Leadership Challenge*. San Francisco: Jossey-Bass.

Kriger, M., and Y. Seng. 2005. "Leadership with Inner Meaning: A Contingency Theory of Leadership Based on the Worldviews of Five Religions." *Leadership Quarterly* 16 (5): 771-806.

Krueger, N. F. 2007. "What Lies Beneath? The Experiential Essence of Entrepreneurial Thinking." *Entrepreneurship Theory and Practice*, January, 123-36.

Kuyper, A. 1931. *Lectures on Calvinism*. Grand Rapids, MI: Wm. B. Eerdmans.

Lawrence, Brother. 1982. *The Practice of the Presence of God*. New Kensington, PA: Whitaker House.

Learned, E. P., A. R. Dooley, and R. L. Katz. 1959. "Personal Values and Business Decisions." *Harvard Business Review* 37: 111-20.

Leavy, B. 2008. "Inspirational Leadership in Business and Other Domains." *Leadership and Business Ethics*. Edited by G. Flynn. Dordrecht: Springer, 103-15.

Lewis, C. S. 1942. *The Screwtape Letters*. New York: HarperCollins.

Lewis, C. S. 1944, 2001. *The Abolition of Man*, San Francisco: HarperCollins.

Lewis, C. S. 1952. *The Voyage of the Dawn Treader*. New York: Macmillan/Collier.

Lewis, R., L. Spears, and B. Lafferty. 2010. "Myers-Briggs and Servant Leadership: The Servant Leader and Personality Type." Ralph Lewis Associates and the Spears Center for Servant-Leadership. Accessed October 14, 2011, at http://spearscenter.org/Myers-BriggsServant-Leadershp-Final.pdf.

Liden, R., B. Erdogan, S. Wayne, and R. Sparrowe. 2006. "Leader-Member Exchange, Differentiation, and Task Interdependence: Implications for Individual and Group Performance." *Journal of Organizational Behavior* 27: 723-46.

Lockwood, A. L. 2009. *The Case for Character Education: A Developmental Approach*. New York: Teachers College, Columbia University.

Louden, R. B. 1984. "On Some Vices of Virtue Ethics." *Virtue Ethics*. Edited by R. Crisp and M. Slote (1987). Oxford: Oxford University Press.

Lussier, R., and C. Achua. 2010. *Leadership: Theory, Application, and Skill Development*. Mason, OH: South-Western Cengage Learning.

Luther, M. 1931. "Against the Robbing and Murdering Hordes of Peasants." *Works of Martin Luther*, vol. IV. Philadelphia: A. J. Holman.

Maak, T., and N. M. Pless, eds. 2006. *Responsible Leadership*. London: Routledge.

Machen, J. G. 1987. *Education, Christianity, and the State*. Jefferson, MD: The Trinity Foundation.

MacIntyre, A. 1985. *After Virtue: A Study in Moral Theory.* London: Duckworth.

Manz, C. C. 1998. *The Leadership Wisdom of Jesus: Practical Lessons for Today.* San Francisco: Berrett-Koehler.

March, J. G., and T. Weil. 2005. *On Leadership.* Oxford: Blackwell.

Marshall, T. 2003. *Understanding Leadership.* Grand Rapids, MI: Baker.

May, W. 1987. "The Virtues of the Business Leader." *The Proceedings of the Second National Consultation on Corporate Ethics, 13-15 May 1987.*

McCain, J. 2011. "Leaders Versus Managers—John McCain's Speech at Tailhook 2011." Accessed October 6, 2011, at http://idreamtalent. com/2011/09/26/leaders-vs-managers-john-mccains-speech -at-tailhook-2011/.

McCoy, B. 2007. *Living into Leadership: A Journey in Ethics.* Stanford, CA: Stanford University Press.

McFaul, T. R. 2003. *Transformation Ethics: Developing the Christian Moral Imagination.* Lanham, MD: University Press of America.

McShulskis, E. 1996. "Coaching Helps but Is Often Not Used." *HR Magazine* 9 (3): 15-16.

Miazza, H. W. 2011. *The Reveille.* Jackson, MS: Camp No. 635 Sons of Confederate Veterans, 3.

Miller, J. R. n.d. "Food for Thought." Unpublished tract.

Miner, J. 2003. "The Rated Importance, Scientific Validity, and Practical Usefulness of Organizational Behavior Theories." *Academy of Management Learning and Education* 2 (3): 250-68.

Mintzberg, H. 1973. *The Nature of Managerial Work.* New York: Harper.

Mitroff, I. and E. Denton. 1999. *A Spiritual Audit of Corporate America.* San Francisco: Jossey-Bass.

Moberg, D. 2008. "Mentoring and Practical Wisdom: Are Mentors Wiser or Just More Politically Skilled?" *Journal of Business Ethics* 83: 835-43.

Moberg, D. J., and M. Velasquez. 2000. "The Ethics of Mentoring." *Business Ethics Quarterly* 14 (1): 95-122.

Nash, L., and S. McLennan. 2001. *Church on Sunday, Work on Monday: The Challenge of Fusing Christian Values with Business Life.* San Francisco: Jossey-Bass.

Naughton, M., and J. R. Cornwall. 2009. "Culture as the Basis of the Good Entrepreneur." *Journal of Religion and Business Ethics* 1 (1): 1-13 (reprint).

Nelson, A. 1996. "Servant Leadership and a Servant versus a Servant Leader." *Leading Your Ministry.* Nashville, TN: Abingdon Press.

Novak, M. 1996. *Business as a Calling: Work and the Examined Life.* New York: The Free Press.

Nutt, P. 1989. "Selecting Tactics to Implement Strategic Plans." *Strategic Management Journal* 10: 145-61.

Paine, L. 1994. "Managing for Organizational Integrity." *Harvard Business Review* 72 (2): 106-17.

Paine, L. 2003. *Value Shift.* New York: McGraw-Hill.

Perkins, W. n.d. "A Treatise on the Vocations or Callings of Men." *Works* 3: 441-76.

Plantinga, C. 2002. *Engaging God's World: A Christian Vision of Faith, Learning, and Living.* Grand Rapids, MI: William B. Eerdmans.

Price, T. L. 2006. *Understanding Ethical Failures in Leadership.* Cambridge, UK: Cambridge University Press.

Pritchard, M. 1998. "Professional Responsibility: Focusing on the Exemplary." *Science and Engineering Ethics* 4 (2): 215-33.

Pruzan, P., and W. Miller. 2006. "Spirituality as the Basis of Responsible Leaders and Responsible Companies." *Responsible Leadership.* Edited by T. Maak and N. Pless. London: Routledge, 68-92.

Rasmussen, T. 1995. "Creating a Culture of Servant-Leadership: A Real-Life Story." *Reflections on Leadership.* Edited by L. Spears. New York: John Wiley & Sons, 282-97.

Raushchenbusch, W. 1912. *Christianizing the Social Order.* New York: Macmillan.

Redpath, Alan. 1954. *Getting to Know the Will of God.* Chicago: InterVarsity.

Rest, J. 1988. "Can Ethics Be Taught in Professional Schools? The Psychological Research." *Ethics: Easier Said than Done* 1: 22-26.

Rest, J., R. Barnett, M. Bebeau, D. Deemer, et al. 1986. *Moral Development: Advances in Research and Theory.* New York: Praeger.

Richardson, J. E., and L. B. McCord. 2000. "Trust in the Marketplace." *Annual Editions: Business Ethics 02/03.* Edited by J. Richardson. Guilford, CT: McGraw-Hill/Dushkin, 106-8.

Roels, Shirley. 1999. *Moving beyond Servant Leadership.* Pasadena, CA: De Pree Leadership Center.

Rouner, L. 1993. "Can Virtue Be Taught in a School? Ivan Illich and Mohandas Gandhi on Deschooling Society." *Can Virtue Be Taught?* Edited by B. Darling-Smith. Notre Dame, IN: University of Notre Dame Press, 139-55.

Ruether, R. 1972. *Liberation Theology*. New York: Paulist Press.

Sandberg, J. 2005. "When Affixing Blame for Inept Managers Go over Their Heads." *The Wall Street Journal*, April 20, B1.

Sanders, J. O. 1994. *Spiritual Leadership*. Chicago: Moody.

Schein, E. 1985. "Organizational Culture: What It Is and How to Change It." *Creating Corporate Culture: From Discord to Harmony*. P. Evans et al., quoted in C. Hampden-Turner (1992). Reading, MA: Addison-Wesley.

Schermerhorn, J. R. 2004. *Core Concepts of Management*. Hoboken, NJ: John Wiley & Sons.

Schumpeter, Joseph. 1950. *Capitalism, Socialism, and Democracy*, 3rd ed. New York: Harper and Brothers.

Scott, D. 1995. *Everyman Revived: The Common Sense of Michael Polanyi*. Grand Rapids, MI: William B. Eerdmans.

Seglin, J. 2005. "The Right Thing: Honesty and the Exit Interview." *New York Times* Syndicate.

Senge, P. 1990. "The Leader's New Work: Building Learning Organizations." *Sloan Management Review* 32 (1): 7-24.

"Shilly-shally: The New President Is Looking Hamstrung Even before He Gets Going." 2007. *The Economist*, July 21, 46-7.

Simonetti, J. L., S. Ariss, and J. Martinez. 1999. "Through the Top with Mentoring." *Business Horizons* 42: 56-61.

Simpson, R. 2006. "Masculinity and Management Education: Feminizing the MBA." *Academy of Management Learning and Education* 5 (2): 182-93.

Sire, J. W. 1997. *The Universe Next Door: A Basic Worldview Catalog*, 3rd ed. Downers Grove, IL: InterVarsity.

Sirico, R. A. 2001. *The Entrepreneurial Vocation.* Grand Rapids, MI: Acton Institute for the Study of Religion and Liberty.

Sison, A. J. G. 2006. "Leadership, Character and Virtues from an Aristotelian Viewpoint." *Responsible Leadership.* Edited by T. Maak and N. M. Pless. London: Routledge, 108-21.

Smith, B., R. Montagno, and T. Kuzmenko. 2004. "Transformational and Servant Leadership: Content and Contextual Comparisons." *Journal of Leadership and Organizational Studies* 10 (4): 80-92.

Smith, F. 1986. *Learning to Lead.* Waco, TX: Word Books.

Solomon, R. 1994. "Business and the Humanities: An Aristotelian Approach to Business Ethics." *Business as a Humanity.* Edited by T.Donaldson and R. E. Freeman. New York: Oxford University Press, 45-75.

Solomon, R. 2003. "Victims of Circumstances? A Defense of Virtue Ethics in Business." *Business Ethics Quarterly* 13(1): 43-62.

Solomon, R. 2005. "Emotional Leadership, Emotional Integrity." *The Quest for Moral Leaders: Essays on Leadership Ethics.* Edited by J. Ciulla, T. Price, and S. Murphy. Cheltenham, Glos., UK: Edward Elgar, 28-44.

Solzhenitsyn, A. 1978. "A World Split Apart" (address at Harvard Class Day Afternoon Exercises, June 8).

Spears, L., ed. 1995. *Reflections on Leadership: How Robert K. Greenleaf's Theory of Servant-Leadership Influenced Today's Top Management Thinkers.* New York: John Wiley & Sons.

Stark, A. 1993. "What's the Matter with Business Ethics?" *Harvard Business Review,* May/June, 38-48.

Stassen, G. H., and D. P. Gushee. 2003. *Kingdom Ethics: Following Jesus in Contemporary Context.* Downers Grove, IL: InterVarsity.

Stewart, R. 1970. *Managers and Their Jobs*. London: Pam Piper.

Swartley, W. M. 2007. "Peacemaking Pillars of Character Formation in the New Testament." *Character Ethics and the New Testament: Moral Dimensions of Scripture*. Edited by R. Brawley. Louisville, KY: Westminster John Knox, 225-43.

Taylor, F. 1916. "The Principles of Scientific Management." *The Great Writings of Management and Organizational Behavior*. Edited by L. Boone and D. Bowen (1987). New York: Random House.

"The Confession of Faith and Catechisms." 2005. *The Westminster Confession of Faith and Catechisms as Adopted by the Orthodox Presbyterian Church*. Willow Grove, PA: The Committee on Christian Education.

The Robert K. Greenleaf Center for Servant Leadership. Accessed June 7, 2011, at http://www.greanleaf.org/leadership/servant-leadership/What-is-Servant Leadership?.

"The Rule of Benedict." 1931. *Christian Ethics: Sources of the Living Tradition*. Edited by W. Beech. New York: The Ronald Press.

Tichy, N. M., and W. G. Bennis. 2007. *Judgment: How Winning Leaders Make Great Calls*. New York: The Penguin Group.

Torrance, T. F. 1984. *Transformation and Convergence in the Frame of Knowledge: Explorations in the Interrelations of Scientific and Theological Enterprise*. Grand Rapids, MI: William B. Eerdmans.

Verstraeten, J. 2008. "Responsible Leadership beyond Managerial Rationality: The Necessity of Reconnecting Ethics and Spirituality." *Leadership and Business Ethics*. Edited by G. Flynn. Dordrecht: Springer, 131-47.

Vroom, V., and A. Jago. 1988. *The New Leadership: Managing Participation in Organizations*. Englewood Cliffs, NJ: Prentice-Hall.

Walsh, B. J., and J. R. Middleton. 1984. *The Transforming Vision: Shaping a Christian Worldview*. Downers Grove, IL: InterVarsity.

Walton, C. 1994. "Management Education: Seeing the Round Earth Squarely." *Business as a Humanity*. Edited by T. Donaldson and R. E. Freeman. New York: Oxford University Press, 109-41.

Walton, Sam, with John Huey. 1992. *Made in America: My Story*. New York: Doubleday.

Weaver, G. R., L. K. Trevino, and B. Agle. 2006. "Some I Look Up To: Ethical Role Models in Organizations." *Organizational Dynamics* 34 (3): 313-30.

Weber, M. 1947. *The Theory of Social and Economic Organization*. Translated by A. M. Henderson and T. Parsons. Edited by T. Parsons. New York: The Free Press.

Wefald, A. J., and J. P. Katz. 2007. "Leaders: The Strategies for Taking Charge." *Academy of Management Perspective* 21 (3): 105-6.

Weiner, B. 1986. *An Attributional Theory of Motivation and Emotion*. New York: Springer-Verlag.

Werhane, Patricia H. 1999. *Moral Imagination and Management Decision Making*. New York: Oxford University Press.

Whetstone, J. T. 1991. "A Revisit of Calvin's Work Ethic: Light for Modern Business" (unpublished Master of Theology thesis, Reformed Theological Seminary).

Whetstone, J. T. 1997. "Ethics and Leadership: Searching for a Comfortable Fit." *Business Ethics: Principles and Practice*. Edited by G. Moore. Sunderland, UK: Business Education Publishers, 81-98.

Whetstone, J. T. 1998. "Teaching Ethics to Managers: Contemporary Problems and a Traditional Solution." *Business Ethics: Perspectives on the Practice of Theory.* Edited by C. Cowton and R. Crisp. Oxford: Oxford University Press, 177-206.

Whetstone, J. T. 2001. "How Virtue Fits within Business Ethics." *Journal of Business Ethics* 3 (2): 101-14.

Whetstone, J. T. 2002. "Personalism and Moral Leadership: The Servant Leader with a Transforming Vision." *Business Ethics: A European Review* 11 (4): 385-92.

Whetstone, J. T. 2003. "The Language of Managerial Excellence: Virtues as Understood and Applied." *Journal of Business Ethics* 44 (3): 343-57.

Whetstone, J. T. 2006. *The Manager as a Moral Person: Exploring Paths to Excellence.* Charlotte, NC: Catawba.

Whetstone, J. T. 2008a. "Practical Wisdom for Living and Working." *Succeed to Lead* 2 (4).

Whetstone, J. T. 2008b. "The Christian's Calling—Even to Entrepreneurial Business." *Contact.* Sioux Center, IA: The International Association for the Promotion of Christian Higher Education, 1-4.

Whetstone, J. T. 2008c. "Honesty and Trust." *Succeed to Lead* 2 (5).

Whetstone, J. T. 2010. "Ethical Mentoring and Character Development" (unpublished paper presented at the Annual Meeting of the Association of Practical and Professional Ethics, Cincinnati, OH, March 5).

Winston, B. E., and K. Patterson. 2006. "An Integrative Definition of Leadership." *International Journal of Leadership Studies* 1 (2): 6-66.

Wojyta, K. 1981. *Toward a Philosophy of Praxis: An Anthology.* Edited by A. Bloch and G. Czuczka. New York: Crossroads Publishing.

Wolterstorff, N. 1976. *Reason within the Bounds of Religion*. Grand Rapids, MI: Eerdmans.

Wolterstorff, N. 1992. "Professorship as a Legitimate Calling." *The Crucible* 2 (3): 19-22.

Yukl, G. 1989. "Managerial Leadership: A Review of Theory and Research." *Journal of Management* 15 (2): 251-89.

Yukl, G. 2010. *Leadership in Organizations,* 7th ed. Upper Saddle River, NJ: Prentice Hall, 419-21.

ABOUT THE AUTHOR

Dr. Whetstone (DPhil, Oxford) is exceptionally qualified to integrate leadership, ethics, and spirituality. He also earned degrees at Washington & Lee U. (B.S.), Sloan School, M.I.T. (M.S. in Management), and Reformed Theological Seminary (M.Div. & Th.M.). An international authority on virtue ethics in business, he has experience in corporate management with two Fortune 500 diversified energy firms, church ministry, university teaching and administration, and leadership in civic organizations. Married with one son, he invests his time in family, writing, and working out.

708 Sarasota Arch
Chesapeake, VA 23322
twhetstone1@cox.net